Company's Coming

Greatest Hits

Biscuits, Muffins & Loaves

visit our **web-site!**
www.companyscoming.com

Over 200 selected recipes by
Jean Paré

Biscuits, Muffins & Loaves

First printing April 1999

Canadian Cataloguing in Publication Data
Paré, Jean
    Greatest Hits: biscuits, muffins & loaves

Issued also in French under title: Jean Paré grands
succès : pains éclair et muffins.
Includes index.
ISBN 1-896891-05-5

    1. Muffins. 2. Cookery (Bread) 3. Biscuits.
I. Title. II. Title: Biscuits, muffins & loaves.
III. Title: Biscuits, muffins and loaves.

TX769.P38 1999   641.8'15   C98-901137-2

Published simultaneously in Canada and the United
States of America by
The Recipe Factory Inc. in conjunction with
Company's Coming Publishing Limited
2311 - 96 Street, Edmonton, Alberta,
Canada T6N 1G3
Tel: 780 • 450-6223
Fax: 780 • 450-1857
www.companyscoming.com

Biscuits, Muffins & Loaves was created thanks to the
dedicated efforts of the people and organizations
listed below.

COMPANY'S COMING PUBLISHING LIMITED

Author	Jean Paré
President	Grant Lovig
V.P., Product Development	Kathy Knowles
Publishing Coordinator	Marlene Crosbie
Production Coordinator	Jaclyn Draker
Copywriting	Debbie Dixon
Design	Nora Cserny
	Jaclyn Draker

THE RECIPE FACTORY INC.

Research & Development Manager	Nora Prokop
Test Kitchen Supervisor	Lynda Elsenheimer
Editor	Stephanie Amodio
Assistant Editor/Food Stylist	Suzanne Hartman
Proofreader	Mimi Tindall
Photographer	Stephe Tate Photo
Prop Stylist	Gabriele McEleney

Color separations, printing, and binding by
Friesens, Altona, Manitoba, Canada
Printed in Canada

FRONT COVER:

1. Cranberry Orange Muffins, page 78
2. Chocolate Filled Muffins, page 73
3. Blueberry Loaf, page 45
4. Whole Wheat Loaf, page 29
5. Brazil Loaf, page 46
6. Cherry Pinwheels, page 21
7. Jam Filled Buns, page 19

Props Courtesy Of:
Chintz & Company, La Cache,
Stokes, The Basket House,
The Glasshouse

visit our web-site!
www.companyscoming.com

table of contents

our cookbooks

COMPANY'S COMING SERIES

150 Delicious Squares
Casseroles
Muffins & More
Salads
Appetizers
Desserts
Soups & Sandwiches
Holiday Entertaining
Cookies
Vegetables
Main Courses
Pasta
Cakes
Barbecues
Dinners of the World
Lunches
Pies
Light Recipes
Microwave Cooking
Preserves
Light Casseroles
Chicken, Etc.
Kids Cooking
Fish & Seafood
Breads
Meatless Cooking
Cooking for Two
Breakfasts & Brunches
Slow Cooker Recipes
Pizza!
One-Dish Meals - NEW
  (August 1999)

SELECT SERIES

Sauces & Marinades
Ground Beef
Beans & Rice
30-Minute Meals
Make-Ahead Salads
No-Bake Desserts

LOW-FAT SERIES

Low-fat Cooking
Low-fat Pasta

GREATEST HITS

Biscuits, Muffins & Loaves
Dips, Spreads & Dressings

INDIVIDUAL TITLES

Company's Coming for Christmas
Easy Entertaining
Beef Today!
Kids - Snacks
Kids - Lunches

the jean paré story

ean Paré grew up understanding that the combination of family, friends and home cooking is the essence of a good life. From her mother she learned to appreciate good cooking, while her father praised even her earliest attempts. When she left home she took with her many acquired family recipes, her love of cooking and her intriguing desire to read recipe books like novels!

In 1963, when her four children had all reached school age, Jean volunteered to cater to the 50th anniversary of the Vermilion School of Agriculture, now Lakeland College. Working out of her home, Jean prepared a dinner for over 1,000 people which launched a flourishing catering operation that continued for over eighteen years. During that time she was provided with countless opportunities to test new ideas with immediate feedback—resulting in empty plates and contented customers! Whether preparing cocktail sandwiches for a house party or serving a hot meal for 1,500 people, Jean Paré earned a reputation for good food, courteous service and reasonable prices.

"Why don't you write a cookbook?" Time and again, as requests for her recipes mounted, Jean was asked that question. Jean's response was to team up with her son, Grant Lovig, in the fall of 1980 to form Company's Coming Publishing Limited. April 14, 1981, marked the debut of 150 DELICIOUS SQUARES, the first Company's Coming cookbook in what soon would become Canada's most popular cookbook series.

Jean Paré's operation has grown steadily from the early days of working out of a spare bedroom in her home. Full-time staff includes marketing personnel located in major cities across Canada. Home Office is based in Edmonton, Alberta in a modern building constructed specially for the company.

Today the company distributes throughout Canada and the United States in addition to numerous overseas markets, all under the guidance of Jean's daughter, Gail Lovig. Best-sellers many times over, Company's Coming cookbooks are published in English and French, plus a Spanish-language edition is available in Mexico. Familiar and trusted in home kitchens the world over, Company's Coming cookbooks are offered in a variety of formats, including the original softcover series.

Jean Paré's approach to cooking has always called for quick and easy recipes using everyday ingredients. Even when travelling, she is constantly on the lookout for new ideas to share with her readers. At home, she can usually be found researching and writing recipes, or working in the company's test kitchen. Jean continues to gain new supporters by adhering to what she calls "the golden rule of cooking": never share a recipe you wouldn't use yourself. It's an approach that works—*millions of times over!*

foreword

hat do the recipes in *Biscuits, Muffins & Loaves* have in common? They are "quick breads", a type of bread that's made without yeast. These popular, easy-to-prepare breads make a welcome addition to any get-together, be it a simple family dinner or afternoon tea with the neighbors. Most of these quick breads can be made ahead. Just prepare the night before, and serve warm and fresh in the morning—or, pull out of the freezer when unexpected company arrives. Add a pot of jam or jelly, or just some margarine or butter, and you're set!

This wide selection of recipes offers you the chance to create something special for breakfast, lunch, dinner, and any other occasion you can think of. Pack a muffin or scone in bag lunches, send a coffee cake to a new neighbor, or take a basket of biscuits to the next church potluck. Biscuits can complement a soup or salad nicely, while fruit loaf is delicious served with a cup of tea or by itself as a light dessert. Sweet rolls go well with a glass of milk or in a school lunch, and a scone makes the perfect companion to your morning coffee.

You can't go wrong serving a selection of these quick breads for just about any occasion. *Biscuits, Muffins & Loaves* is packed with over 200 recipes, each one a true winner. Try them all; you'll find it difficult to pick your favorites!

each recipe

has been analyzed using the most updated version of the Canadian Nutrient File from Health and Welfare Canada, which is based upon the United States Department of Agriculture (USDA) Nutrient Data Base.

Margaret Ng, B.Sc. (Hon), M.A.
Registered Dietician

Biscuits

Complement any meal with the smell and flavor of homemade biscuits. Enjoy *Whole Wheat Biscuits*, page 9, with fresh fruit in the morning, or nibble on *Confetti Biscuits*, page 8, when sipping your afternoon tea. *Savory Sausage Biscuits*, page 13, are perfect to serve with your favorite soup. And, for an extra special touch with dessert, indulge a sweet tooth with *Fancy Crescents*, page 15.

BISCUIT LIPS

Fun biscuits to serve with any soup. Serve right from the oven and you have hot lips!

All-purpose flour	**2 cups**	**500 mL**
Baking powder	**4 tsp.**	**20 mL**
Granulated sugar	**2 tbsp.**	**30 mL**
Salt	**1 tsp.**	**5 mL**
Hard margarine (or butter)	**$^1/_3$ cup**	**75 mL**
Milk	**$^3/_4$ cup**	**175 mL**
Hard margarine (or butter), for spreading	**$2^1/_2$ tbsp.**	**37 mL**

Mix first 4 ingredients in medium bowl. Cut in margarine until mixture is crumbly.

Add milk. Stir with fork until dough forms ball. Add bit more milk if necessary to make soft dough. Knead 10 times on lightly floured surface. Pat or roll out $^1/_4$ inch (6 mm) thick. Cut into $2^3/_4$ inch (7 cm) rounds. Cut through center of each with sharp knife to barely score surface.

Spread with margarine. Fold over (margarine inside) and press edges together. Arrange on greased baking sheet. Bake in 425°F (220°C) oven for 8 to 10 minutes until risen and nicely browned. Makes about 20 biscuits.

1 biscuit: 98 Calories; 4.7 g Total Fat; 197 mg Sodium; 2 g Protein; 12 g Carbohydrate; trace Dietary Fiber

Pictured on page 17.

CRUNCHY DROP BISCUITS

When you haven't time to roll and cut, this is it.

All-purpose flour	3 cups	750 mL
Granulated sugar	2 tbsp.	30 mL
Baking powder	5 tsp.	25 mL
Salt	1 tsp.	5 mL
Hard margarine (or butter)	¹/₂ cup	125 mL
Large egg	1	1
Milk	1 cup	250 mL

Combine flour, sugar, baking powder and salt in large bowl. Cut in margarine until mixture is crumbly. Make a well in center.

Beat egg with spoon in small bowl. Add milk. Pour into well in flour mixture. Stir lightly to mix. Batter should be sticky. Stir in 1 tbsp. (15 mL) milk at a time until it is. Drop batter by teaspoonfuls onto ungreased baking sheet. Or form into circle to bake; break off a mound to eat. Bake in 450°F (230°C) oven for 10 to 12 minutes until browned. Makes 15 to 20 biscuits.

1 biscuit: 175 Calories; 7.3 g Total Fat; 276 mg Sodium; 4 g Protein; 23 g Carbohydrate; 1 g Dietary Fiber

HERB BISCUITS

Definite dill flavor with a hint of onion. Traditional "layered" look. Combine dry ingredients in the morning or night before, or make biscuits ahead and freeze.

All-purpose flour	2 cups	500 mL
Granulated sugar	2 tsp.	10 mL
Baking powder	1 tbsp.	15 mL
Salt	¹/₂ tsp.	2 mL
Parsley flakes	¹/₂ tsp.	2 mL
Chopped chives	1 tsp.	5 mL
Dill weed	¹/₂ tsp.	2 mL
Cooking oil	3 tbsp.	50 mL
Milk	²/₃ cup	150 mL

Measure first 7 ingredients into medium bowl. Stir. Make a well in center.

Add cooking oil and milk. Stir just to moisten. Knead 6 to 8 times on lightly floured surface. Pat or roll out ³/₄ inch (2 cm) thick. Cut into 2 inch (5 cm) rounds. Arrange on ungreased baking sheet. Bake in 400°F (205°C) oven for about 15 minutes. Makes 12 biscuits.

1 biscuit: 121 Calories; 3.8 g Total Fat; 125 mg Sodium; 3 g Protein; 19 g Carbohydrate; 1 g Dietary Fiber

CONFETTI BISCUITS

Fruity and very good. A special treat for tea or lunch.

All-purpose flour	2¹/₂ cups	625 mL
Cream of tartar	1¹/₂ tsp.	7 mL
Baking soda	³/₄ tsp.	4 mL
Salt	³/₄ tsp.	4 mL
Hard margarine (or butter)	¹/₄ cup	60 mL
Cut glazed mixed fruit, finely chopped	¹/₂ cup	125 mL
Milk	1 cup	250 mL

Combine flour, cream of tartar, baking soda and salt in medium bowl. Stir together well. Cut in margarine until mixture is mealy.

Add fruit and milk. Stir to form soft ball. Knead about 6 times on lightly floured surface. Pat or roll out ³/₄ inch (2 cm) thick. Cut into 2 inch (5 cm) rounds. Arrange on greased baking sheet. Bake in 450°F (230°C) oven for 10 to 12 minutes until risen and browned. Makes 16 biscuits.

1 biscuit: 130 Calories; 3.5 g Total Fat; 274 mg Sodium; 3 g Protein; 22 g Carbohydrate; 1 g Dietary Fiber

Pictured on page 35.

DROP CHEESE BISCUITS

Speckled with cheese. These are so easy to prepare.

All-purpose flour	2 cups	500 mL
Granulated sugar	1 tbsp.	15 mL
Baking powder	4 tsp.	20 mL
Salt	1/4 tsp.	1 mL
Grated light sharp Cheddar cheese	1 1/2 cups	375 mL
Cooking oil	2 tbsp.	30 mL
Skim milk	1 cup	250 mL

Measure first 5 ingredients into medium bowl. Stir together well.

Add cooking oil and milk. Stir just to moisten. Drop by tablespoonfuls onto baking sheet that has been sprayed with no-stick cooking spray. Bake in 425°F (220°C) oven for 12 to 15 minutes. Makes 16 biscuits.

1 biscuit: 120 Calories; 4.2 g Total Fat; 127 mg Sodium; 5 g Protein; 15 g Carbohydrate; 1 g Dietary Fiber

Pictured on page 89.

HERBED BISCUITS

A just-right flavored biscuit. Excellent with an egg or tuna filling.

All-purpose flour	1 1/2 cups	375 mL
Baking powder	1 tbsp.	15 mL
Granulated sugar	2 tsp.	10 mL
Paprika	1/2 tsp.	2 mL
Ground oregano	1 1/2 tsp.	7 mL
Chili powder	3/4 tsp.	4 mL
Salt	1/2 tsp.	2 mL
Pepper	1/4 tsp.	1 mL
Grated sharp Cheddar cheese	3/4 cup	175 mL
Cooking oil	1/4 cup	60 mL
Milk	1/2 cup	125 mL

Stir first 9 ingredients together in small bowl.

Add cooking oil and milk. Stir to form soft ball. Turn out onto lightly floured surface. Knead gently 6 to 8 times. Roll out 3/8 inch (1 cm) thick. Cut into 1 1/4 inch (3 cm) rounds. Arrange on ungreased baking sheet. Bake in 400°F (205°C) oven for about 12 minutes until risen and browned. Cool on rack. Makes about 24 biscuits.

1 biscuit: 72 Calories; 3.8 g Total Fat; 86 mg Sodium; 2 g Protein; 7 g Carbohydrate; trace Dietary Fiber

WHOLE WHEAT BISCUITS

Looks so different from the usual white. So good! They look like little loaves of bread.

Whole wheat flour	2 cups	500 mL
Baking powder	1 tbsp.	15 mL
Salt	1/4 tsp.	1 mL
Cooking oil	2 tbsp.	30 mL
Cooking (not fancy) molasses	1 tbsp.	15 mL
Skim milk	3/4 cup	175 mL

Stir flour, baking powder and salt together in medium bowl.

Add cooking oil, molasses and milk. Stir to form soft dough. Knead 8 times on lightly floured surface. Pat or roll out 3/4 inch (2 cm) thick. Cut into 1 x 2 inch (2.5 x 5 cm) rectangles. Arrange on ungreased baking sheet. Bake in 425°F (220°C) oven for 12 to 15 minutes. Makes 19 biscuits.

1 biscuit: 65 Calories; 1.7 g Total Fat; 44 mg Sodium; 2 g Protein; 11 g Carbohydrate; 2 g Dietary Fiber

CORNY BISCUITS

Cornmeal gives these good little biscuits a bit of a crunch.

Cornmeal	³⁄₄ cup	175 mL
Onion flakes	1 tbsp.	15 mL
Skim milk	³⁄₄ cup	175 mL
Biscuit mix	2 cups	500 mL

Combine cornmeal, onion flakes and milk in medium bowl. Let stand for 10 minutes.

Add biscuit mix. Stir to form soft dough. Knead 6 to 8 times on lightly floured surface. Roll out ³⁄₄ inch (2 cm) thick. Cut into 2 inch (5 cm) rounds. Arrange on ungreased baking sheet. Bake in 400°F (205°C) oven for 15 minutes until browned. Makes 15 biscuits.

1 biscuit: 96 Calories; 2.3 g Total Fat; 219 mg Sodium; 2 g Protein; 17 g Carbohydrate; 1 g Dietary Fiber

CORN BISCUITS

A tender drop biscuit. Cream-style corn provides the liquid used. These freeze well.

Biscuit mix	1¹⁄₂ cups	375 mL
Canned cream-style corn	1 cup	250 mL
Hard margarine (or butter), melted	¹⁄₂ cup	125 mL

Stir biscuit mix and corn together in small bowl.

Drop by teaspoonfuls into margarine. Turn to coat. Arrange on ungreased baking sheet. Bake in 400°F (205°C) oven for 15 to 20 minutes until risen and browned. Makes about 12 biscuits.

1 biscuit: 154 Calories; 9.7 g Total Fat; 371 mg Sodium; 2 g Protein; 16 g Carbohydrate; 1 g Dietary Fiber

CHILI BISCUITS

These surprising biscuits have a burnt orange color.

All-purpose flour	2 cups	500 mL
Baking powder	1 tbsp.	15 mL
Salt	³⁄₄ tsp.	4 mL
Chili powder	1 tsp.	5 mL
Onion powder	1¹⁄₂ tsp.	7 mL
Hard margarine (or butter)	³⁄₄ cup	175 mL
Grated sharp Cheddar cheese	1 cup	250 mL
Tomato juice	³⁄₄ cup	175 mL

Combine first 5 ingredients in large bowl. Cut in margarine until mixture is crumbly.

Stir in cheese and tomato juice until dough forms soft ball. Knead 8 to 10 times on lightly floured surface. Pat or roll out ³⁄₄ inch (2 cm) thick. Cut into 2 inch (5 cm) rounds. Arrange on greased baking sheet. Bake in 425°F (220°C) oven for about 12 minutes until browned. Serve warm. Makes 16 biscuits.

1 biscuit: 177 Calories; 11.9 g Total Fat; 329 mg Sodium; 4 g Protein; 14 g Carbohydrate; 1 g Dietary Fiber

Pictured on page 71.

PASTRY BISCUITS

These look like cookies but taste like biscuits. Serve with jam or jelly.

Hard margarine (or butter), softened	¹⁄₂ cup	125 mL
Cream cheese, softened	4 oz.	125 g
All-purpose flour	1 cup	250 mL

Cream margarine and cream cheese together well in medium bowl. Mix in flour. Shape into 1 roll about 1¹⁄₂ inches (3.8 cm) in diameter and 7 inches (18 cm) long. Roll up in waxed paper. Chill all day or overnight. Cut into ¹⁄₄ inch (6 mm) slices. Place on ungreased baking sheet. Bake in 400°F (205°C) oven for about 10 minutes until browned. Makes about 24 biscuits.

1 biscuit: 75 Calories; 6 g Total Fat; 63 mg Sodium; 1 g Protein; 4 g Carbohydrate; trace Dietary Fiber

RAISIN BISCUITS

Nice flaky layer. Serve cold with cheese slices or warm with butter or jam.

All-purpose flour	3 cups	750 mL
Granulated sugar	2 tbsp.	30 mL
Cream of tartar	2 tsp.	10 mL
Baking powder	1 tbsp.	15 mL
Baking soda	1 tsp.	5 mL
Salt	1 tsp.	5 mL
Ground cinnamon	$1/2$-1 tsp.	2-5 mL
Hard margarine (or butter)	$1/2$ cup	125 mL
Raisins (or currants)	1 cup	250 mL
Milk	$1^1/3$ cups	325 mL

Measure first 7 ingredients into large bowl. Stir together well.

Cut in margarine until mixture is crumbly.

Add raisins and milk. Stir with fork to form soft ball. Knead 8 to 10 times on lightly floured surface. Pat or roll out dough 1 inch (2.5 cm) thick. Cut into $2^1/2$ inch (6.4 cm) rounds. Arrange about 2 inches (5 cm) apart on greased baking sheet. Bake in 425°F (220°C) oven for 20 to 30 minutes until risen and browned. Makes 18 biscuits.

1 biscuit: 169 Calories; 5.9 g Total Fat; 345 mg Sodium; 3 g Protein; 26 g Carbohydrate; 1 g Dietary Fiber

Pictured on page 53 and on back cover.

BISCUITS

Soft, flaky texture. Just right with jam or jelly.

All-purpose flour	2 cups	500 mL
Baking powder	2 tsp.	10 mL
Salt	$1/2$ tsp.	2 mL
Hard margarine (or butter)	3 tbsp.	50 mL
Baking soda	$1/2$ tsp.	2 mL
Buttermilk	1 cup	250 mL

Combine first 3 ingredients in medium bowl. Cut in margarine until mixture is crumbly.

Stir baking soda into buttermilk in small bowl. Add to flour mixture. Mix until dough forms ball. Knead 8 to 10 times on lightly floured surface. Pat or roll out into circle $1/2$ to $3/4$ inch (12 to 20 mm) thick. Cut into 2 inch (5 cm) rounds. Place 1 inch (2.5 cm) apart on greased baking sheet. Bake in 450°F (230°C) oven for 10 to 12 minutes. Makes 16 biscuits.

1 biscuit: 87 Calories; 2.5 g Total Fat; 173 mg Sodium; 2 g Protein; 14 g Carbohydrate; 1 g Dietary Fiber

GLUTEN-FREE BISCUITS

Quick and easy. Best eaten warm.

Rice flour	1 cup	250 mL
Potato starch	$3/4$ cup	175 mL
Granulated sugar	2 tsp.	10 mL
Gluten-free baking powder	2 tsp.	10 mL
Salt	$1/4$ tsp.	1 mL
Xanthan gum (optional)	1 tsp.	5 mL
Hard margarine (or butter)	$1/4$ cup	60 mL
Water (or milk)	$2/3$ cup	150 mL

Measure first 6 ingredients into medium bowl. Stir together well.

Cut in margarine until mixture is crumbly.

Add water. Stir until dough forms ball. Knead 6 to 8 times on rice-floured surface. Pat or roll out 1 inch (2.5 cm) thick. Cut into 2 inch (5 cm) rounds. Arrange on greased baking sheet. Bake in 350°F (175°C) oven for about 15 minutes. These do not brown much. Makes 10 biscuits.

1 biscuit: 160 Calories; 5.3 g Total Fat; 134 mg Sodium; 2 g Protein; 26 g Carbohydrate; 1 g Dietary Fiber

CURRANT BISCUITS: Add $1/4$ cup (60 mL) currants to dough.

CHEESE BISCUITS: Add $1/3$ cup (75 mL) grated sharp Cheddar cheese to dough.

RAISIN ORANGE BISCUITS

A great accompaniment to tea. Combine and cover the orange peel and raisins in the morning. Raisins will help keep peel soft. Or, make biscuits ahead and freeze.

All-purpose flour	2 cups	500 mL
Granulated sugar	2 tbsp.	30 mL
Baking powder	4 tsp.	20 mL
Salt	1/2 tsp.	2 mL
Hard margarine (or butter)	1/4 cup	60 mL
Grated orange peel	1 tbsp.	15 mL
Raisins	1/2 cup	125 mL
Large egg, fork-beaten	1	1
Milk	1/2 cup	125 mL

Measure first 5 ingredients into medium bowl. Cut in margarine until mixture is crumbly.

Add orange peel and raisins. Stir together well.

Add egg and milk. Stir to form soft ball. Knead 6 times on lightly floured surface. Pat or roll out 3/4 inch (2 cm) thick. Cut into 2 inch (5 cm) rounds. Arrange on ungreased baking sheet. Bake in 425°F (220°C) oven for about 12 minutes. Makes 16 biscuits.

1 biscuit: 120 Calories; 3.8 g Total Fat; 141 mg Sodium; 3 g Protein; 19 g Carbohydrate; 1 g Dietary Fiber

Pictured on page 35.

Serve quick breads piled in a napkin-lined wicker basket or arranged on a pretty china plate. Use bright colors to liven up less colorful baked goods.

BISCUITS WITH HERBS

Serve this flavor-rich biscuit with any main course.

All-purpose flour	1 cup	250 mL
Whole wheat flour	1 cup	250 mL
Baking powder	4 tsp.	20 mL
Salt	1/2 tsp.	2 mL
Dill weed	1/2 tsp.	2 mL
Ground thyme	1/4 tsp.	1 mL
Garlic powder	1/8 tsp.	0.5 mL
Granulated sugar	1 tbsp.	15 mL
Hard margarine (or butter)	1/4 cup	60 mL
Milk	3/4 cup	175 mL

Measure first 8 ingredients into medium bowl. Mix well. Cut in margarine until mixture is crumbly.

Pour milk over top. Stir until mixture forms soft ball. Knead 6 to 8 times on lightly floured surface. Pat or roll out 3/4 inch (2 cm) thick. Cut into 2 inch (5 cm) rounds. Arrange on ungreased baking sheet. Bake in 450°F (230°C) oven for 12 to 15 minutes. Makes 12 biscuits.

1 biscuit: 126 Calories; 4.7 g Total Fat; 169 mg Sodium; 3 g Protein; 18 g Carbohydrate; 2 g Dietary Fiber

LOCKER BISCUITS

Davey Jones must have had these in his locker on the ocean floor. Baked in tiny tart pans, these rise high to the occasion.

Biscuit mix	3 cups	750 mL
Granulated sugar	3 tbsp.	50 mL
Cold beer	1 1/4 cups	300 mL

Mix all 3 ingredients in medium bowl. Dough will be very soft. Fill greased tiny tart pans to the top. Bake in 450°F (230°C) oven for 12 to 15 minutes until risen and browned. Makes 30 biscuits.

1 biscuit: 67 Calories; 1.7 g Total Fat; 176 mg Sodium; 1 g Protein; 11 g Carbohydrate; trace Dietary Fiber

BRAN BISCUITS

Good with a salad meal or just coffee or tea.

All-purpose flour	2 cups	500 mL
Granulated sugar	1/4 cup	60 mL
Baking powder	4 tsp.	20 mL
Salt	1/2 tsp.	2 mL
Hard margarine (or butter)	1/2 cup	125 mL
Flakes of bran cereal	1/2 cup	125 mL
Chopped dates	1/2 cup	125 mL
Large egg	1	1
Milk	3/4 cup	175 mL

Combine flour, sugar, baking powder and salt in large bowl. Cut in margarine until mixture is crumbly. Stir in cereal and dates. Make a well in center.

Beat egg in small bowl until frothy. Mix in milk. Pour into well in flour mixture. Stir lightly to form soft dough. Add more milk if needed. Dough should be sticky. Drop by tablespoonfuls 1 inch (2.5 cm) apart onto greased baking sheet. Bake in 450°F (230°C) oven for 10 to 12 minutes. Makes 16 biscuits.

1 biscuit: 158 Calories; 6.8 g Total Fat; 186 mg Sodium; 3 g Protein; 22 g Carbohydrate; 1 g Dietary Fiber

SAVORY SAUSAGE BISCUITS

Serve this "meal in a biscuit" with soup. Excellent.

Sausage meat	1/2 lb.	225 g
All-purpose flour	2 cups	500 mL
Baking powder	2 tsp.	10 mL
Baking soda	1/2 tsp.	2 mL
Salt	1 tsp.	5 mL
Hard margarine (or butter)	1/4 cup	60 mL
Buttermilk	3/4 cup	175 mL

Scramble-fry sausage meat in frying pan. Drain very well. Set aside.

Combine flour, baking powder, baking soda and salt in large bowl. Cut in margarine until mixture is crumbly. Stir in sausage meat. Make a well in center.

Pour buttermilk into well in flour mixture. Stir quickly to form soft dough. Turn out onto lightly floured surface. Knead 8 to 10 times. Pat or roll out 3/4 inch (2 cm) thick. Cut into rounds, squares or triangles. Place on ungreased baking sheet. Bake in 450°F (230°C) oven for 12 to 15 minutes until browned. Makes 12 to 15 biscuits.

1 biscuit: 159 Calories; 7.7 g Total Fat; 423 mg Sodium; 4 g Protein; 18 g Carbohydrate; 1 g Dietary Fiber

BANNOCK BISCUITS MODERN

A different biscuit to be sure. Cooked in a modern appliance rather than over a fire.

Whole wheat flour	1 1/2 cups	375 mL
Cornmeal	1/2 cup	125 mL
Baking powder	1 tbsp.	15 mL
Salt	1/2 tsp.	2 mL
Skim milk	1 1/2 cups	375 mL
Granulated sugar	2 tbsp.	30 mL

Stir first 4 ingredients together in medium bowl.

Add milk and sugar. Stir just to moisten. Mixture should be thick and barely spreadable. Spray frying pan with no-stick cooking spray. Spread about 1/4 cup (60 mL) batter in flattish circle. An ice-cream scoop is ideal for this. Try one first to be sure pan isn't too hot. An electric frying pan would be 325°F (160°C). Cover. Cook for about 9 minutes without turning. Tops will feel dry and firm and bottoms will be browned. Makes 10 large biscuits.

1 biscuit: 108 Calories; 0.6 g Total Fat; 163 mg Sodium; 4 g Protein; 23 g Carbohydrate; 3 g Dietary Fiber

WHOLE MEAL BISCUITS

More like a crispy cracker than a biscuit. Sweet, but with the wheat and oat flavors coming through. These freeze well.

Whole wheat flour	1⅓ cups	325 mL
Quick-cooking rolled oats (not instant)	⅓ cup	75 mL
Brown sugar, packed	⅓ cup	75 mL
Baking powder	1 tsp.	5 mL
Salt	½ tsp.	2 mL
Hard margarine (or butter), softened	6 tbsp.	100 mL
Milk	¼ cup	60 mL

Combine first 5 ingredients in medium bowl. Cut in margarine until mixture is crumbly.

Add milk. Mix well. Add bit more if needed to hold together to roll. Roll out to ¼ inch (6 mm) thickness on lightly floured surface. Cut into 3 inch (7.5 cm) rounds. Arrange on greased baking sheet. Bake in 350°F (175°C) oven for 20 to 25 minutes until lightly browned. Makes 12 biscuits.

1 biscuit: 136 Calories; 6.3 g Total Fat; 189 mg Sodium; 3 g Protein; 18 g Carbohydrate; 2 g Dietary Fiber

FLAKY BISCUITS

Great served with jam or marmalade. Have dry ingredients ready the night before or make biscuits ahead and freeze.

All-purpose flour	2 cups	500 mL
Baking powder	1 tbsp.	15 mL
Baking soda	¼ tsp.	1 mL
Salt	½ tsp.	2 mL
Hard margarine (or butter)	¼ cup	60 mL
Plain yogurt	¾ cup	175 mL
Milk	¼ cup	60 mL

Measure first 5 ingredients into medium bowl. Cut in margarine until mixture is crumbly.

Add yogurt and milk. Stir to form soft ball. Knead 6 times on lightly floured surface. Pat or roll out ¾ inch (2 cm) thick. Cut into 2½ inch (6.4 cm) rounds. Arrange on ungreased baking sheet. Bake in 375°F (190°C) oven for 10 to 12 minutes. Makes 12 biscuits.

1 biscuit: 131 Calories; 4.6 g Total Fat; 208 mg Sodium; 3 g Protein; 19 g Carbohydrate; 1 g Dietary Fiber

LOADED BISCUITS

Full flavored biscuits to round out any meal. Quick and easy.

All-purpose flour	2 cups	500 mL
Granulated sugar	2 tbsp.	30 mL
Baking powder	4 tsp.	20 mL
Salt	1 tsp.	5 mL
Grated sharp Cheddar cheese	1¼ cups	300 mL
Finely chopped green onion	3 tbsp.	50 mL
Finely chopped green pepper	2 tbsp.	30 mL
Cooking oil	⅓ cup	75 mL
Milk	¾ cup	175 mL

Measure flour, sugar, baking powder and salt into medium bowl. Stir well. Add cheese, green onion and green pepper. Stir together lightly.

Add cooking oil and milk. Stir to form soft ball. Turn out onto lightly floured surface. Knead 8 to 10 times. Pat or roll out to ¾ inch (2 cm) thickness. Cut with 2 inch (5 cm) round floured cookie cutter. Arrange on ungreased baking sheet. Bake in 425°F (220°C) oven for about 15 minutes until browned. Makes 12 biscuits.

1 biscuit: 204 Calories; 10.9 g Total Fat; 318 mg Sodium; 6 g Protein; 21 g Carbohydrate; 1 g Dietary Fiber

Pictured on page 71.

FANCY CRESCENTS

Rich little things that melt in your mouth.

All-purpose flour	2 cups	500 mL
Hard margarine (or butter)	1 cup	250 mL
Egg yolk (large)	1	1
Sour cream	¾ cup	175 mL
Granulated sugar	¼ cup	60 mL
Ground cinnamon	1 tsp.	5 mL

Measure flour into large bowl. Cut in margarine until mixture is crumbly.

Beat egg yolk and sour cream together in small bowl with spoon. Add to flour mixture. Mix well. Cover. Chill for at least 4 hours or overnight.

Combine sugar and cinnamon in small cup. Sprinkle some over working surface. Use instead of extra flour for rolling dough. Roll about ¼ to ⅓ of dough into circle about 10 inches (25 cm) in diameter. Sprinkle sugar mixture on both sides as needed, considering taste as well as ease of rolling. Cut into 16 wedges. Beginning at outside of each edge, roll toward center. Arrange on ungreased baking sheet close together but not touching. Bake in 375°F (190°C) oven for 25 to 30 minutes until browned. Makes 4 dozen crescents.

1 crescent: 68 Calories; 4.8 g Total Fat; 50 mg Sodium; 1 g Protein; 6 g Carbohydrate; trace Dietary Fiber

Pictured on page 53 and on back cover.

MAYONNAISE BISCUITS

So few ingredients. So easy.

All-purpose flour	2 cups	500 mL
Baking powder	4 tsp.	20 mL
Salt	¾ tsp.	4 mL
Salad dressing (or mayonnaise)	¼ cup	60 mL
Milk	¾ cup	175 mL

Stir flour, baking powder and salt together in medium bowl. Make a well in center.

Pour salad dressing and milk into well in flour mixture. Stir until soft ball forms. Pat or roll out on lightly floured surface. Cut into 2 inch (5 cm) rounds. Place on ungreased baking sheet. Bake in 425°F (220°C) oven for 12 minutes until browned. Makes 12 biscuits.

1 biscuit: 115 Calories; 2.9 g Total Fat; 216 mg Sodium; 3 g Protein; 19 g Carbohydrate; 1 g Dietary Fiber

POTATO BISCUITS

Very moist. Serve warm with your favorite casserole.

All-purpose flour	1½ cups	375 mL
Baking powder	1 tbsp.	15 mL
Salt	½ tsp.	2 mL
Granulated sugar	1 tbsp.	15 mL
Skim milk	⅔ cup	150 mL
Cooked mashed potato	1 cup	250 mL
Cooking oil	3 tbsp.	50 mL

Measure first 4 ingredients into medium bowl. Stir together.

Add remaining 3 ingredients. Stir until soft ball forms. Knead 6 or 8 times on lightly floured surface. Roll out ¾ inch (2 cm) thick. Cut into 2 inch (5 cm) rounds. Arrange on baking sheet sprayed with no-stick cooking spray. Bake in 425°F (220°C) oven for 15 minutes until risen and lightly browned. Makes 16 biscuits.

1 biscuit: 80 Calories; 2.7 g Total Fat; 94 mg Sodium; 2 g Protein; 12 g Carbohydrate; 1 g Dietary Fiber

STICKY CHEESE BISCUITS

These are a yummy looking biscuit with the cheese clinging to the tops.

All-purpose flour	2 cups	500 mL
Baking powder	4 tsp.	20 mL
Granulated sugar	1 tsp.	5 mL
Salt	¾ tsp.	4 mL
Hard margarine (or butter)	¼ cup	60 mL
Milk	⅔ cup	150 mL
Hard margarine (or butter)	½ cup	125 mL
Grated medium Cheddar cheese	1 cup	250 mL

Measure first 4 ingredients into medium bowl. Cut in first amount of margarine until mixture is crumbly.

Stir in milk until soft ball forms. Knead 6 to 8 times on lightly floured surface. Pat or roll out dough ¾ inch (2 cm) thick. Cut straight down with 1¾ inch (4.5 cm) round floured cookie cutter. Arrange in ungreased 8 × 8 inch (20 × 20 cm) pan. Line with foil for easy cleanup.

Melt second amount of margarine in small saucepan. Cool slightly. Add cheese. Stir together well. Spoon over each biscuit. Bake in 425°F (220°C) oven for 12 to 15 minutes. Makes 16 biscuits.

1 biscuit: 179 Calories; 11.9 g Total Fat; 291 mg Sodium; 4 g Protein; 14 g Carbohydrate; 1 g Dietary Fiber

ONION BISCUITS

The onion flavor comes from dry soup mix. So easy. These freeze well.

All-purpose flour	2 cups	500 mL
Granulated sugar	1 tbsp.	15 mL
Baking powder	4 tsp.	20 mL
Salt	½ tsp.	2 mL
Envelope dry onion soup mix (stir before dividing)	½ × 1½ oz.	½ × 42 g
Hard margarine (or butter), softened	⅓ cup	75 mL
Milk	¾ cup	175 mL

Combine all 7 ingredients in medium bowl. Stir until mixture forms soft ball. Pat or roll out ¾ inch (2 cm) thick on lightly floured surface. Cut into 1¾ inch (4.5 cm) rounds. Arrange on ungreased baking sheet. Bake in 425°F (220°C) oven for 12 to 15 minutes until risen and browned. Makes about 16 biscuits.

1 biscuit: 110 Calories; 4.4 g Total Fat; 261 mg Sodium; 2 g Protein; 15 g Carbohydrate; 1 g Dietary Fiber

1. Biscuit Lips, page 7
2. Savory Onion Bread, page 43
3. Apple Streusel Muffins, page 66
4. Cinnamon Treats, page 19
5. Tomato Herb Bread, page 30
6. Chipper Muffins, page 87
7. Cranberry Coffee Cake, page 25

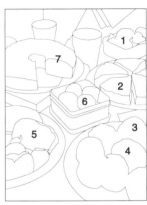

Props Courtesy Of: Dansk Gifts

Buns

Satisfy your sweet tooth with these quick buns. Include extra special *Jam-Filled Buns*, page 19, or *Jiffy Cinnamon Rolls*, page 18, the next time you host brunch for your family or friends. *Cherry Pinwheels*, page 21, are perfect to pack in a school or work lunch to spoil your loved ones.

JIFFY CINNAMON ROLLS

Something so easy shouldn't be so good. A single recipe won't be enough.

All-purpose flour	2 cups	500 mL
Granulated sugar	2 tbsp.	30 mL
Baking powder	4 tsp.	20 mL
Salt	1 tsp.	5 mL
Hard margarine (or butter)	1/4 cup	60 mL
Milk	1 cup	250 mL
Hard margarine (or butter), softened	1/3 cup	75 mL
Brown sugar, packed	1 cup	250 mL
Ground cinnamon	1 tbsp.	15 mL
Currants (or cut up raisins)	1/3 cup	75 mL
GLAZE		
Icing (confectioner's) sugar	1/2 cup	125 mL
Milk, for thinning		

Combine flour, sugar, baking powder and salt in large bowl. Cut in first amount of margarine until mixture is crumbly. Make a well in center.

Pour milk into well in flour mixture. Stir to form soft dough, adding bit more milk if needed. Turn out onto lightly floured surface. Knead 8 to 10 times. Roll out into rectangle about 1/3 inch (1 cm) thick and 12 inches (30 cm) long. Width will vary.

Cream second amount of margarine, brown sugar and cinnamon together well. Drop by teaspoonfuls into each of 12 greased muffin cups. Spread remaining cinnamon mixture over dough rectangle. Sprinkle currants over top. Roll up as for jelly roll. Mark first, then cut, into 12 slices. Place, cut side down, in muffin cups. Bake in 400°F (205°C) oven for 20 to 25 minutes. Turn out onto tray.

Glaze: Mix icing sugar with enough milk to make barely pourable consistency. Drizzle over cinnamon rolls. Makes 12 rolls.

1 roll: 290 Calories; 10 g Total Fat; 361 mg Sodium; 3 g Protein; 48 g Carbohydrate; 1 g Dietary Fiber

CINNAMON TREATS

Not sweet but a pleasant nutty flavor with a hint of cinnamon. Glaze adds the finishing sweet touch.

All-purpose flour	2 cups	500 mL
Granulated sugar	1 tbsp.	15 mL
Baking powder	1 tbsp.	15 mL
Salt	1/2 tsp.	2 mL
Hard margarine (or butter)	1/2 cup	125 mL
Milk	3/4 cup	175 mL
FILLING		
Ground pecans	1/2 cup	125 mL
Brown sugar, packed	1/2 cup	125 mL
Ground cinnamon	2 tsp.	10 mL
Hard margarine (or butter), melted	1 tbsp.	15 mL
GLAZE		
Icing (confectioner's) sugar	3/4 cup	175 mL
Milk	4 tsp.	20 mL
Vanilla	1/8 tsp.	0.5 mL

Measure first 4 ingredients into large bowl. Cut in margarine until mixture is crumbly.

Add milk. Stir to form soft ball. Knead 8 times on lightly floured surface. Pat or roll out into 10 x 15 inch (25 x 38 cm) rectangle.

Filling: Mix pecans, brown sugar and cinnamon in small bowl.

Brush dough with margarine. Sprinkle with cinnamon mixture, keeping about 1/2 inch (12 mm) in from edges. Roll up from long side. Pinch seam to seal. Cut into 20 slices, 3/4 inch (2 cm) thick. Arrange on greased baking sheet, placing about 1 inch (2.5 cm) apart. Bake in 400°F (205°C) oven for 12 to 14 minutes until lightly browned.

Glaze: Stir icing sugar, milk and vanilla together in small bowl, adding more icing sugar or milk as needed to make barely pourable consistency. Drizzle, in pinwheel fashion, over buns while still warm. Makes 20 buns.

1 bun: 161 Calories; 7.4 g Total Fat; 133 mg Sodium; 2 g Protein; 20 g Carbohydrate; 1 g Dietary Fiber

Pictured on page 17.

JAM-FILLED BUNS

These perky little buns disappear in a flash.

All-purpose flour	2 cups	500 mL
Granulated sugar	2 tbsp.	30 mL
Baking powder	1 tbsp.	15 mL
Salt	1/2 tsp.	2 mL
Hard margarine (or butter)	1/2 cup	125 mL
Large egg	1	1
Milk	1/2 cup	125 mL
Raspberry jam		

Combine flour, sugar, baking powder and salt in large bowl. Cut in margarine until mixture is crumbly. Make a well in center.

Beat egg with fork in small bowl until light and frothy. Stir in milk. Pour, all at once, into well in flour mixture. Stir lightly to form soft dough. Add more milk if needed. Knead dough 8 to 10 times on lightly floured surface. Pat or roll out 3/4 inch (2 cm) thick. Using 2 inch (5 cm) round cookie cutter, push straight down to cut. Arrange well apart on greased baking sheet.

Make a deep hollow in center in top of each biscuit. Drop small spoonful of jam into each hollow. Bake in 450°F (230°C) oven for 12 to 15 minutes. Serve hot. Makes 14 to 16 buns.

1 bun: 158 Calories; 7.6 g Total Fat; 192 mg Sodium; 3 g Protein; 19 g Carbohydrate; 1 g Dietary Fiber

Pictured on front cover.

FUN BUNS

A bit fussy but not difficult to make. These will disappear fast.

All-purpose flour	2 cups	500 mL
Granulated sugar	3 tbsp.	50 mL
Baking powder	4 tsp.	20 mL
Cream of tartar	1/2 tsp.	2 mL
Salt	1/2 tsp.	2 mL
Hard margarine (or butter)	1/4 cup	60 mL
Milk	3/4 cup	175 mL
COATING		
Brown sugar, packed	6 tbsp.	100 mL
Ground cinnamon	2 tsp.	10 mL
Hard margarine (or butter)	1 tbsp.	15 mL

Measure first 5 ingredients into medium bowl. Stir together well. Cut in first amount of margarine until mixture is crumbly.

Add milk. Stir until mixture pulls away from side of bowl and forms soft ball. Turn out onto lightly floured surface. Knead 8 times until dough is smooth. Cut dough into 2 equal portions. Cut each portion in half, making 4 pieces of dough. Divide each piece into 3, making total of 12 pieces. Roll out each piece into long rope at least 12 inches (30 cm) long.

Coating: Measure brown sugar and cinnamon into small bowl. Stir together well. Sprinkle onto working surface. Spread into 4 x 14 inch (10 x 35 cm) rectangle.

Melt second amount of margarine in small saucepan on medium. Remove from heat. Use pastry brush to brush margarine into another rectangle on working surface, same size as sugar-cinnamon rectangle. Roll 1 rope at a time in margarine, then in sugar-cinnamon, to coat. Roll up like spiral or pinwheel, like a snake might curl up. Pinch last 1/2 inch (12 mm) of end flat and tuck underneath bun. Arrange buns on greased baking sheet. Bake on center rack in 400°F (205°C) oven for 12 to 15 minutes. Wooden pick inserted in several buns should come out clean. Makes 12 buns.

1 bun: 173 Calories; 5.4 g Total Fat; 203 mg Sodium; 3 g Protein; 28 g Carbohydrate; 1 g Dietary Fiber

Pictured on page 89.

When warming buns in the microwave oven, remember that you can always add time but you can't take it away. An overheated bun (particularly a sweet bun) will be chewy and tough as it cools.

CHERRY PINWHEELS

Flavored with almonds, these sweet rolls are just right with coffee or tea.

All-purpose flour	4½ cups	1.1 L
Granulated sugar	½ cup	125 mL
Baking powder	2 tbsp.	30 mL
Salt	1¼ tsp.	6 mL
Hard margarine (or butter)	¾ cup	175 mL
Small orange, cut and seeded, with peel	1	1
Large egg	1	1
Large eggs	2	2
Sour cream	1 cup	250 mL
Almond flavoring	1 tsp.	5 mL
Ground almonds	¼ cup	60 mL
Chopped glazed cherries	⅔ cup	150 mL
Finely chopped candied ginger (optional)	⅔ cup	150 mL
FILLING		
Hard margarine (or butter), softened	3 tbsp.	50 mL
Granulated sugar	¼ cup	60 mL
Ground nutmeg	2 tsp.	10 mL
GLAZE		
Icing (confectioner's) sugar	1 cup	250 mL
Milk (or water)	1 tbsp.	15 mL
Vanilla	¼ tsp.	1 mL
Cherries and almonds		

Measure first 4 ingredients into large bowl. Cut in margarine until mixture is crumbly.

Place orange and 1 egg in blender. Process until orange is ground.

Add next 2 eggs, sour cream and flavoring. Process to mix.

Add almonds, cherries and ginger to flour mixture. Add blender contents. Stir to form soft ball. Turn out onto lightly floured surface. Knead 6 to 8 times. Roll out to 24 x 14 inch (60 x 35 cm) rectangle.

Filling: Spread dough with margarine. Stir sugar and nutmeg together in small bowl. Sprinkle over margarine. Roll up from long side like a jelly roll. Cut into 18 slices. Place on greased baking sheet. Bake in 375°F (190°C) oven for about 25 minutes.

Glaze: Mix first 3 ingredients in small cup to make a barely pourable glaze. Drizzle over buns. Sprinkle with cherries and almonds if desired. Makes 18 buns.

1 bun: 324 Calories; 14.1 g Total Fat; 331 mg Sodium; 5 g Protein; 45 g Carbohydrate; 1 g Dietary Fiber

Pictured on front cover.

TEA BUNS

Rich and raisiny. A snap to make.

All-purpose flour	2 cups	500 mL
Granulated sugar	⅓ cup	75 mL
Baking powder	4 tsp.	20 mL
Salt	¾ tsp.	4 mL
Hard margarine (or butter)	½ cup	125 mL
Raisins	1 cup	250 mL
Large egg	1	1
Milk	¾ cup	175 mL

Combine flour, sugar, baking powder and salt in large bowl. Cut in margarine until mixture is crumbly. Stir in raisins. Make a well in center.

Beat egg lightly with spoon in small bowl. Stir in milk. Pour into well in flour mixture. Stir to make soft dough. Pat or roll out ¾ inch (2 cm) thick on lightly floured surface. Cut with biscuit cutter into 2 inch (5 cm) rounds. Place on ungreased baking sheet. Bake in 400°F (205°C) oven for 20 minutes until brown. Makes 12 to 16 buns.

1 bun: 229 Calories; 9 g Total Fat; 286 mg Sodium; 4 g Protein; 34 g Carbohydrate; 1 g Dietary Fiber

Coffee Cakes

*a*re you wondering what to serve to unexpected afternoon or evening company? With these coffee cake recipes, you won't have to worry any longer. Make them ahead of time and keep in your freezer until needed. Simply defrost, warm in the oven if desired, and serve. *Sour Cream Coffee Cake*, page 26, goes nicely with morning coffee, while *Blueberry Streusel Cake*, page 22, is ideal for a luncheon dessert.

BLUEBERRY STREUSEL CAKE

Wrap well and freeze ahead of time. Take out the night before your brunch. Heat just before serving.

Hard margarine (or butter), softened	½ cup	125 mL
Granulated sugar	¾ cup	175 mL
Large eggs	3	3
Vanilla	1 tsp.	5 mL
Milk	1 cup	250 mL
All-purpose flour	3 cups	750 mL
Baking powder	1 tbsp.	15 mL
Ground cinnamon	1½ tsp.	7 mL
Ground nutmeg	1 tsp.	5 mL
Salt	1 tsp.	5 mL
Fresh blueberries (or frozen, thawed)	3 cups	750 mL
STREUSEL TOPPING		
All-purpose flour	¾ cup	175 mL
Quick-cooking rolled oats (not instant)	¾ cup	175 mL
Brown sugar, packed	¾ cup	175 mL
Hard margarine (or butter)	½ cup	125 mL

Cream margarine and sugar together in large bowl. Beat in eggs, 1 at a time. Add vanilla and milk. Mix.

Add flour, baking powder, cinnamon, nutmeg and salt. Stir slowly to moisten. Continue to stir until smooth. Spread in greased 9 × 13 inch (22 × 33 cm) pan.

Sprinkle with blueberries.

Streusel Topping: Measure flour, rolled oats and brown sugar into small bowl. Cut in margarine until mixture is crumbly. Spread over blueberries. Bake in 350°F (175°C) oven for 40 to 50 minutes. Cuts into 15 pieces.

1 piece: 380 Calories; 15 g Total Fat; 365 mg Sodium; 6 g Protein; 56 g Carbohydrate; 2 g Dietary Fiber

Pictured on page 35.

CHERRY CREAM COFFEE CAKE

A moist white cake with a pretty red layer beneath a not too sweet topping. In fact you may even want to add more brown sugar when you make it for the second time.

Hard margarine (or butter), softened	¹/₂ cup	125 mL
Granulated sugar	1 cup	250 mL
Large eggs	2	2
Sour cream	1 cup	250 mL
Vanilla	1 tsp.	5 mL
All-purpose flour	2 cups	500 mL
Baking powder	1¹/₂ tsp.	7 mL
Baking soda	1 tsp.	5 mL
Salt	¹/₄ tsp.	1 mL
Canned cherry pie filling	19 oz.	540 mL
TOPPING		
Brown sugar, packed	¹/₂ cup	125 mL
All-purpose flour	³/₄ cup	175 mL
Ground cinnamon	1 tsp.	5 mL
Hard margarine (or butter), softened	¹/₃ cup	75 mL
Salt	¹/₄ tsp.	1 mL

Cream margarine and sugar together in medium bowl. Beat in eggs, 1 at a time. Mix in sour cream and vanilla.

Sift in flour, baking powder, baking soda and salt. Stir just to moisten. Scrape into greased 9 x 13 inch (22 x 33 cm) pan. Use wet hand to pat smooth.

Spread pie filling over top.

Topping: Mix all 5 ingredients in small bowl until crumbly. Sprinkle over pie filling. Bake in 350°F (175°C) oven for 40 to 45 minutes until wooden pick inserted near center comes out clean. Serve immediately. Cuts into 15 pieces.

1 piece: 350 Calories; 14.1 g Total Fat; 329 mg Sodium; 4 g Protein; 53 g Carbohydrate; 1 g Dietary Fiber

ORANGE COFFEE CAKE

Serve fresh and warm for a splendid snack.

Hard margarine (or butter), softened	¹/₄ cup	60 mL
Granulated sugar	¹/₂ cup	125 mL
Large eggs	2	2
Vanilla	1 tsp.	5 mL
Grated orange peel	2 tbsp.	30 mL
Juice from 1 orange, plus water to make	³/₄ cup	175 mL
All-purpose flour	2 cups	500 mL
Baking powder	1 tbsp.	15 mL
Salt	¹/₂ tsp.	2 mL
TOPPING		
Hard margarine (or butter)	3 tbsp.	50 mL
Brown sugar, packed	¹/₃ cup	75 mL
All-purpose flour	¹/₄ cup	60 mL
Ground cinnamon	1 tsp.	5 mL

Cream margarine and sugar together well in small bowl. Beat in eggs, 1 at a time. Add vanilla, orange peel and orange juice. Stir together.

Add flour, baking powder and salt. Stir just to moisten. Turn into greased 9 x 9 inch (22 x 22 cm) pan.

Topping: Melt margarine in small saucepan. Stir in brown sugar, flour and cinnamon. Mix well. Sprinkle over top of batter. Bake in 375°F (190°C) oven for 25 to 30 minutes until wooden pick inserted near center comes out clean. Serve warm. Cuts into 12 pieces.

1 piece: 229 Calories; 7.9 g Total Fat; 210 mg Sodium; 4 g Protein; 36 g Carbohydrate; 1 g Dietary Fiber

DUTCH APPLE CAKE

Apple slices are layered over top of the batter and covered with a crumb mixture. Serve warm or cold with whipped cream for a sure hit.

Hard margarine (or butter), softened	¹/₂ cup	125 mL
Granulated sugar	¹/₄ cup	60 mL
Large egg	1	1
Brandy flavoring	1¹/₂ tsp.	7 mL
All-purpose flour	1¹/₄ cups	300 mL
Baking powder	1¹/₂ tsp.	7 mL
Salt	¹/₂ tsp.	2 mL
Milk	²/₃ cup	150 mL
Cooking apples (such as McIntosh), peeled and cut into eights	3-4	3-4
TOPPING		
Hard margarine (or butter), melted	3 tbsp.	50 mL
Brown sugar, packed (or granulated sugar)	¹/₂ cup	125 mL
All-purpose flour	¹/₄ cup	60 mL
Ground cinnamon	1 tsp.	5 mL

Cream margarine, sugar and egg together in medium bowl until smooth. Add brandy flavoring.

Mix flour, baking powder and salt in small bowl.

Add flour mixture to margarine mixture in 3 additions, alternately with milk in 2 additions, beginning and ending with flour mixture. Spread in greased 8 × 8 inch (20 × 20 cm) pan.

Arrange apple slices in rows over top to cover.

Topping: Mix all 4 ingredients in small bowl. Sprinkle over apples. Bake in 375°F (190°C) oven for about 30 minutes until apples are tender. Cuts into 9 pieces.

1 piece: 325 Calories; 15.6 g Total Fat; 344 mg Sodium; 4 g Protein; 43 g Carbohydrate; 2 g Dietary Fiber

RHUBARB COFFEE CAKE

What spring treat could be better? It's worth inviting company over for this alone.

Hard margarine (or butter)	¹/₂ cup	125 mL
Granulated sugar	1¹/₂ cups	375 mL
Large eggs	2	2
Sour cream	1 cup	250 mL
Vanilla	1 tsp.	5 mL
All-purpose flour	2 cups	500 mL
Baking soda	1 tsp.	5 mL
Finely cut fresh rhubarb	2 cups	500 mL
TOPPING		
Brown sugar, packed	¹/₂ cup	125 mL
All-purpose flour	1 tbsp.	15 mL
Ground cinnamon	1 tsp.	5 mL
Hard margarine (or butter), softened	1 tbsp.	15 mL

Cream margarine and sugar together in medium bowl. Beat in eggs, 1 at a time. Stir in sour cream and vanilla.

Mix flour and baking soda in small bowl. Fold into batter.

Stir in rhubarb. Turn into greased 9 × 13 inch (22 × 33 cm) pan.

Topping: Mix all 4 ingredients in small bowl until crumbly. Sprinkle over top. Bake in 350°F (175°C) oven for 30 to 40 minutes until wooden pick inserted in center comes out clean. Cuts into 15 pieces.

1 piece: 281 Calories; 10.5 g Total Fat; 196 mg Sodium; 3 g Protein; 44 g Carbohydrate; 1 g Dietary Fiber

CRANBERRY COFFEE CAKE

Whether you try cranberries, raspberries or blueberries you will have a very colorful treat.

All-purpose flour	2 cups	500 mL
Granulated sugar	1/2 cup	125 mL
Baking powder	1 tbsp.	15 mL
Salt	1/2 tsp.	2 mL
Large eggs	2	2
Cooking oil	1/4 cup	60 mL
Milk	3/4 cup	175 mL
Cranberries (fresh or frozen)	1 cup	250 mL
TOPPING		
All-purpose flour	1/3 cup	75 mL
Brown sugar, packed	1/3 cup	75 mL
Hard margarine (or butter)	1/4 cup	60 mL
Ground cinnamon	1 tsp.	5 mL

Mix flour, sugar, baking powder and salt in large bowl.

Beat eggs together in small bowl until frothy. Mix in cooking oil and milk. Pour into flour mixture. Mix.

Fold in cranberries. Scrape into greased 10 inch (25 cm) tube pan.

Topping: Mix flour, brown sugar, margarine and cinnamon in small bowl. Sprinkle over top of batter. Bake in 350°F (175°C) oven for 50 to 60 minutes or until it begins to pull away from sides of pan. Cool in pan for 30 minutes. Remove from pan to rack to cool completely. Turn right side up. Cuts into 16 pieces.

1 piece: 192 Calories; 7.7 g Total Fat; 140 mg Sodium; 3 g Protein; 28 g Carbohydrate; 1 g Dietary Fiber

Pictured on page 17.

BLUEBERRY COFFEE CAKE: Omit cranberries. Add 1 cup (250 mL) blueberries, fresh or frozen.

RASPBERRY COFFEE CAKE: Omit cranberries. Add 1 cup (250 mL) raspberries, fresh or frozen.

CHOCO COFFEE CAKE

No cinnamon in this. Delicious chocolate chips instead.

Hard margarine (or butter), softened	1/2 cup	125 mL
Granulated sugar	1 cup	250 mL
Large eggs	2	2
Vanilla	1 tsp.	5 mL
All-purpose flour	2 cups	500 mL
Baking powder	1 tsp.	5 mL
Baking soda	1 tsp.	5 mL
Sour cream	1 cup	250 mL
Semisweet chocolate chips	1/2 cup	125 mL
TOPPING		
Brown sugar, packed	1/2 cup	125 mL
All-purpose flour	1/2 cup	125 mL
Cocoa	2 tsp.	10 mL
Hard margarine (or butter), softened	1/4 cup	60 mL
Semisweet chocolate chips	1/2 cup	125 mL
Finely chopped nuts	1/2 cup	125 mL

Cream margarine, sugar and 1 egg together well in large bowl. Beat in remaining egg and vanilla. Add flour, baking powder, baking soda and sour cream. Stir together well. Stir in chocolate chips. Turn into greased 9 x 13 inch (22 x 33 cm) pan. Smooth top.

Topping: Mix brown sugar, flour, cocoa and margarine until crumbly. Stir in chocolate chips and nuts. Sprinkle over top of batter. Bake in 350°F (175°C) oven for 45 minutes until wooden pick inserted near center comes out clean. Cuts into 15 pieces.

1 piece: 365 Calories; 19.2 g Total Fat; 227 mg Sodium; 5 g Protein; 46 g Carbohydrate; 2 g Dietary Fiber

SOUR CREAM COFFEE CAKE

M-m-m-marvelous. Will become a company favorite. Best served warm.

Hard margarine (or butter), softened	½ cup	125 mL
Granulated sugar	¾ cup	175 mL
Large eggs	3	3
Vanilla	1 tsp.	5 mL
All-purpose flour	2 cups	500 mL
Baking powder	1 tsp.	5 mL
Baking soda	1 tsp.	5 mL
Salt	½ tsp.	2 mL
Low-fat sour cream	1 cup	250 mL
CRUMB MIX		
Brown sugar, packed	1 cup	250 mL
Ground cinnamon	2 tsp.	10 mL
Hard margarine (or butter), softened	6 tbsp.	100 mL
Chopped walnuts (or pecans)	¾ cup	175 mL

Cream margarine and sugar together in large bowl. Beat in eggs, 1 at a time. Add vanilla. Mix.

Stir flour, baking powder, baking soda and salt together in small bowl.

Add flour mixture to egg mixture in 3 additions, alternately with sour cream in 2 additions, beginning and ending with flour mixture.

Crumb Mix: Mix brown sugar, cinnamon and margarine in small bowl until crumbly.

Add walnuts. Stir well. Spread ½ of batter in greased 10 inch (25 cm) tube pan. Sprinkle with ½ of crumb mix. Drop remaining ½ of batter by small spoonfuls over top. Smooth as best you can. Sprinkle remaining ½ of crumb mix over top. Bake in 350°F (175°C) oven for about 45 minutes until wooden pick inserted in center comes out clean. Cuts into 16 pieces.

1 piece: 314 Calories; 16.5 g Total Fat; 302 mg Sodium; 4 g Protein; 39 g Carbohydrate; 1 g Dietary Fiber

Pictured on page 89.

FRUITED COFFEE CAKE

A tasty change from traditional coffee cake.

Large egg	1	1
Granulated sugar	¾ cup	175 mL
Hard margarine (or butter), softened	½ cup	125 mL
All-purpose flour	1½ cups	375 mL
Baking powder	2 tsp.	10 mL
Salt	½ tsp.	2 mL
Milk	½ cup	125 mL
Cut glazed mixed fruit	¼ cup	60 mL
Currants	¼ cup	60 mL
Raisins	¼ cup	60 mL
Brown sugar, packed	¼ cup	60 mL
Ground cinnamon	½ tsp.	2 mL

Beat egg, sugar and margarine together well.

Stir flour, baking powder and salt together in small bowl.

Add flour mixture in 3 additions, alternately with milk in 2 additions, beginning and ending with flour mixture. Stir just to moisten.

Fold in glazed fruit, currants and raisins. Turn into greased 9 x 9 inch (22 x 22 cm) pan.

Mix brown sugar and cinnamon in small cup. Sprinkle over top. Bake in 350°F (175°C) oven for 25 to 30 minutes until wooden pick inserted in center comes out clean. Cuts into 9 pieces.

1 piece: 327 Calories; 11.8 g Total Fat; 303 mg Sodium; 4 g Protein; 53 g Carbohydrate; 1 g Dietary Fiber

Loaves

ea loaves or fruit loaves, as they are often called, are as much a part of afternoon tea as the tea itself! They are also popular at wedding or baby showers and on most buffet tables. For an interesting variety of colors and flavors, try combining different loaves on one platter. Tantalize your guests with *Chocolate Orange Bread*, page 27, or *Apricot Raisin Loaf*, page 31. *Brazil Loaf*, page 46, is so colorful, while decadent *Raspberry Cream Muffins*, page 79, are sure to please. For a more hearty loaf, bake a batch of *Boston Brown Bread*, page 52, or *Southern Corn Bread*, page 30.

CHOCOLATE ORANGE BREAD

Rich golden brown loaf with chocolate chips well distributed. Not too sweet. Make ahead, without glaze, and freeze. Glaze on day of serving.

Large egg	1	1
Cooking oil	1/3 cup	75 mL
Granulated sugar	2/3 cup	150 mL
Prepared orange juice	1 cup	250 mL
Grated peel of 1 medium orange		
All-purpose flour	2 cups	500 mL
Baking powder	1 tbsp.	15 mL
Salt	1/2 tsp.	2 mL
Semisweet chocolate chips	2/3 cup	150 mL
ORANGE GLAZE		
Icing (confectioner's) sugar	1 cup	250 mL
Prepared orange juice	2 tbsp.	30 mL

Beat egg, cooking oil and sugar together well in large bowl. Add orange juice and orange peel. Mix well.

Sift flour, baking powder and salt over top. Stir just to moisten.

Add chocolate chips. Stir. Turn into greased 9 x 5 x 3 inch (22 x 12.5 x 7.5 cm) loaf pan. Bake in 350°F (175°C) oven for about 1 hour until wooden pick inserted in center comes out clean. Cool in pan for 15 minutes. Remove from pan to rack to cool completely.

Orange Glaze: Mix icing sugar and orange juice, adding more or less juice to make proper consistency. Drizzle over loaf. Cuts into 18 slices.

1 slice: 194 Calories; 7.1 g Total Fat; 83 mg Sodium; 2 g Protein; 32 g Carbohydrate; 1 g Dietary Fiber

STRAWBERRY LOAF

Use frozen berries to make this moist tasty loaf.

All-purpose flour	2 cups	500 mL
Granulated sugar	1 cup	250 mL
Ground cinnamon	1 tsp.	5 mL
Baking soda	½ tsp.	2 mL
Salt	½ tsp.	2 mL
Large eggs	2	2
Cooking oil	½ cup	125 mL
Frozen sliced strawberries in syrup, thawed, drained, syrup reserved	15 oz.	425 g
Reserved strawberry syrup	½ cup	125 mL
Chopped pecans (or walnuts)	½ cup	125 mL

Thoroughly mix first 5 ingredients in large bowl. Make a well in center.

Beat eggs in small bowl until frothy. Pour into well in flour mixture along with cooking oil.

Add strawberries, reserved syrup and pecans. Stir just to moisten. Turn into greased 9 × 5 × 3 inch (23 × 12.5 × 7.5 cm) loaf pan. Bake in 350°F (175°C) oven for about 1 hour until wooden pick inserted in center comes out clean. Cool in pan for 10 minutes. Remove from pan to rack to cool completely. Cuts into 18 slices.

1 slice: 209 Calories; 9.5 g Total Fat; 122 mg Sodium; 3 g Protein; 30 g Carbohydrate; 1 g Dietary Fiber

ZUCCHINI PINEAPPLE LOAF

This good loaf is large and tender.

Large eggs	2	2
Cooking oil	½ cup	125 mL
Granulated sugar	1 cup	250 mL
Grated zucchini, with peel	1 cup	250 mL
Canned crushed pineapple, drained	½ cup	125 mL
Vanilla	1 tsp.	5 mL
All-purpose flour	2 cups	500 mL
Baking soda	1 tsp.	5 mL
Baking powder	½ tsp.	2 mL
Salt	½ tsp.	2 mL
Ground cinnamon	¾ tsp.	4 mL
Ground nutmeg	¼ tsp.	1 mL
Chopped walnuts	½ cup	125 mL

Beat eggs, cooking oil and sugar together in large bowl. Stir in zucchini, pineapple and vanilla.

Measure remaining 7 ingredients into small bowl. Stir together well. Pour all at once into batter. Stir just to moisten. Pour into greased 9 × 5 × 3 inch (22 × 12.5 × 7.5 cm) loaf pan. Bake in 350°F (175°C) oven for 1 hour until wooden pick inserted in center comes out clean. Cool in pan for 10 minutes. Remove from pan to rack to cool completely. Cuts into 18 slices.

1 slice: 192 Calories; 9.4 g Total Fat; 160 mg Sodium; 3 g Protein; 25 g Carbohydrate; 1 g Dietary Fiber

Variation: Add 1 cup (250 mL) raisins.

Cool loaves completely, then slice and lay individual slices on baking sheet. Freeze. When frozen, wrap together and re-freeze. Take out one slice or several slices as needed.

SOUR MILK QUICK BREAD

No yeast in this. A good flavored loaf. Excellent toasted.

All-purpose flour	4 cups	1 L
Cream of tartar	2 tsp.	10 mL
Baking soda	1 tsp.	5 mL
Granulated sugar	1 tsp.	5 mL
Salt	½ tsp.	2 mL
Large egg, fork-beaten	1	1
Cooking oil	2 tbsp.	30 mL
Sour milk (1½ tbsp., 25 mL, white vinegar plus milk to make)	1½ cups	375 mL

Measure flour, cream of tartar, baking soda, sugar and salt into large bowl. Stir together.

Add egg, cooking oil and sour milk. Stir to mix well. Dough will be sticky. Turn into greased 9 x 5 x 3 inch (22 x 12.5 x 7.5 cm) loaf pan. Bake in 350°F (175°C) oven for 45 to 55 minutes, rotating pan at half-time. Cuts into 18 slices.

1 slice: 134 Calories; 2.3 g Total Fat; 206 mg Sodium; 4 g Protein; 24 g Carbohydrate; 1 g Dietary Fiber

WHOLE WHEAT LOAF

Does not contain yeast. Quick to prepare. This freezes well.

Whole wheat flour	2 cups	500 mL
All-purpose flour	1 cup	250 mL
Granulated sugar	⅓ cup	75 mL
Baking soda	1 tsp.	5 mL
Salt	1 tsp.	5 mL
Buttermilk	2 cups	500 mL

Measure first 5 ingredients into medium bowl. Mix well.

Add buttermilk. Stir just to moisten. Turn into greased 9 x 5 x 3 inch (22 x 12.5 x 7.5 cm) loaf pan. Bake in 375°F (190°C) oven for 55 to 65 minutes until wooden pick inserted in center comes out clean. Let stand for 2 to 3 minutes. Remove from pan to rack to cool. Cuts into 16 slices.

1 slice: 114 Calories; 0.7 g Total Fat; 290 mg Sodium; 4 g Protein; 24 g Carbohydrate; 2 g Dietary Fiber

Pictured on front cover.

CRANBERRY LOAF

Almost tangy, you will wish this small loaf was huge.

All-purpose flour	1 cup	250 mL
Graham cracker crumbs	1 cup	250 mL
Brown sugar, packed	½ cup	125 mL
Baking powder	2 tsp.	10 mL
Salt	½ tsp.	2 mL
Chopped cranberries (fresh or frozen)		
Raisins	1 cup	250 mL
Chopped walnuts	½ cup	125 mL
Grated orange peel	1 tbsp.	15 mL
Large egg, fork-beaten	1	1
Prepared orange juice	1 cup	250 mL
Cooking oil	⅓ cup	75 mL

Mix first 5 ingredients in large bowl.

Stir in cranberries, raisins, walnuts and orange peel.

Add egg, orange juice and cooking oil. Stir until blended. Scrape into greased 9 x 5 x 3 inch (22 x 12.5 x 7.5 cm) loaf pan. Bake in 350°F (175°C) oven for 1 hour until wooden pick inserted in center comes out clean. Cool in pan for 10 minutes. Remove from pan to rack to cool completely. Cuts into 18 slices.

1 slice: 177 Calories; 7.6 g Total Fat; 127 mg Sodium; 3 g Protein; 27 g Carbohydrate; 1 g Dietary Fiber

SOUTHERN CORN BREAD

Makes a nice change. Serve warm with lunch or evening meal.

All-purpose flour	1 cup	250 mL
Cornmeal	1 cup	250 mL
Granulated sugar	⅓ cup	75 mL
Baking powder	2½ tsp.	12 mL
Baking soda	¼ tsp.	1 mL
Salt	¼ tsp.	1 mL
Milk	1 cup	250 mL
White vinegar	1 tbsp.	15 mL
Hard margarine (or butter), melted	6 tbsp.	100 mL
Large egg, fork-beaten	1	1

Stir first 6 ingredients together in medium bowl.

Measure milk into small cup. Stir in vinegar. Let stand for 5 minutes. Add to flour mixture. Stir together.

Add margarine and egg. Stir together. Turn into greased 9 x 9 inch (22 x 22 cm) pan. Bake in 400°F (205°C) oven for about 20 minutes until wooden pick inserted near center comes out clean. Cuts into 12 pieces.

1 piece: 175 Calories; 6.8 g Total Fat; 165 mg Sodium; 3 g Protein; 25 g Carbohydrate; 1 g Dietary Fiber

PEANUT BUTTER LOAF

A light peanut butter flavor. Not overpowering. Freezes well.

Large egg	1	1
Granulated sugar	½ cup	125 mL
Smooth peanut butter	½ cup	125 mL
Milk	1¼ cups	300 mL
All-purpose flour	2 cups	500 mL
Baking powder	4 tsp.	20 mL
Salt	1 tsp.	5 mL

Beat egg in medium bowl. Add sugar and peanut butter. Beat together. Slowly mix in milk.

Stir flour, baking powder and salt together in small bowl. Add to peanut butter mixture. Stir just to moisten. Turn into greased 9 x 5 x 3 inch (22 x 12.5 x 7.5 cm) loaf pan, being sure to push into corners. Bake in 350°F (175°C) oven for about 1 hour until wooden pick inserted near center comes out clean. Cool in pan for 10 minutes. Remove from pan to rack to cool completely. Cuts into 18 slices.

1 slice: 133 Calories; 4.4 g Total Fat; 203 mg Sodium; 4 g Protein; 20 g Carbohydrate; 1 g Dietary Fiber

TOMATO HERB BREAD

A good spice combination. Easy and tasty.

All-purpose flour	3 cups	750 mL
Baking powder	4 tsp.	20 mL
Granulated sugar	1 tbsp.	15 mL
Dried whole oregano	½ tsp.	2 mL
Dried sweet basil	½ tsp.	2 mL
Salt	½ tsp.	2 mL
Tomato juice	1½ cups	375 mL
Hard margarine (or butter), melted	¼ cup	60 mL

Combine first 6 ingredients in large bowl. Stir. Make a well in center.

Pour tomato juice and margarine into well in flour mixture. Stir just to moisten. Turn into greased 9 x 5 x 3 inch (22 x 12.5 x 7.5 cm) loaf pan. Bake in 400°F (205°C) oven for 35 to 40 minutes until wooden pick inserted near center comes out clean. If loaf appears to be browning too much, lay a piece of foil over top. Remove from pan to rack to cool. Cuts into 16 slices.

1 slice: 124 Calories; 3.1 g Total Fat; 207 mg Sodium; 3 g Protein; 21 g Carbohydrate; 1 g Dietary Fiber

Pictured on page 17.

POPPY SEED LOAF

Make it with or without cherries, with or without the glaze. It is good either way.

Poppy seed	¼ cup	60 mL
Milk	¾ cup	175 mL
Hard margarine (or butter), softened	½ cup	125 mL
Granulated sugar	¾ cup	175 mL
Large eggs	2	2
Lemon juice	1 tsp.	5 mL
All-purpose flour	2 cups	500 mL
Baking powder	2½ tsp.	12 mL
Salt	½ tsp.	2 mL
Maraschino cherries, well drained and halved	½ cup	125 mL

Add poppy seed to milk in small bowl. Let stand for 30 minutes.

Combine margarine, sugar and 1 egg in medium bowl. Beat together well. Add remaining egg and lemon juice. Beat until smooth. Stir in poppy seed mixture.

Measure flour, baking powder, salt and cherries into small bowl. Mix well. Stir into batter just to moisten. Pour into greased 9 x 5 x 3 inch (22 x 12.5 x 7.5 cm) loaf pan. Bake in 350°F (175°C) oven for 1 hour. Cool in pan for 10 minutes. Remove from pan to rack to cool completely. Cuts into 18 slices.

1 slice: 169 Calories; 7.3 g Total Fat; 160 mg Sodium; 3 g Protein; 23 g Carbohydrate; 1 g Dietary Fiber

Pictured on page 53 and on back cover.

APRICOT RAISIN LOAF

A super loaf, flavorful and fruity. Make a day ahead for easier cutting and better flavor.

Hard margarine (or butter), softened	¼ cup	60 mL
Brown sugar, packed	¾ cup	175 mL
Large eggs	2	2
Prepared orange juice	1 cup	250 mL
All-purpose flour	2 cups	500 mL
Baking powder	2 tsp.	10 mL
Salt	1 tsp.	5 mL
Coarsely chopped dried apricots	1 cup	250 mL
Raisins	1 cup	250 mL
Chopped pecans (or walnuts)	½ cup	125 mL
Finely grated orange peel	1 tbsp.	15 mL
GLAZE		
Apricot jam	3 tbsp.	50 mL
Water	1 tbsp.	15 mL

Beat margarine, brown sugar and 1 egg together in large bowl until smooth. Beat in remaining egg. Blend in orange juice.

Measure flour, baking powder and salt into small bowl. Stir in apricots, raisins, pecans and orange peel. Pour all at once over egg mixture. Stir just to moisten. Scrape into greased 9 x 5 x 3 inch (22 x 12.5 x 7.5 cm) loaf pan. Bake in 350°F (175°C) oven for 1 hour until wooden pick inserted in center comes out clean. Cool in pan for 10 minutes. Remove from pan to rack to cool completely.

Glaze: Heat apricot jam and water. Put through strainer. Spoon over hot loaf. Cuts into 18 slices.

1 slice: 206 Calories; 5.9 g Total Fat; 197 mg Sodium; 3 g Protein; 37 g Carbohydrate; 2 g Dietary Fiber

DATE LOAF

Extra moist, extra yummy.

Chopped dates	1¼ cups	300 mL
Boiling water	¾ cup	175 mL
Baking soda	1 tsp.	5 mL
Large egg	1	1
Brown sugar, packed	¾ cup	175 mL
Salt	¾ tsp.	4 mL
Vanilla	1 tsp.	5 mL
All-purpose flour	1½ cups	375 mL
Baking powder	1 tsp.	5 mL
Chopped walnuts	½ cup	125 mL
Hard margarine (or butter), melted	¼ cup	60 mL

Combine dates, boiling water and baking soda in small bowl. Stir to cool.

Beat egg lightly in large bowl. Add brown sugar, salt and vanilla. Beat together. Stir in date mixture.

Mix flour and baking powder in medium bowl. Pour into date mixture. Stir to mix. Stir in walnuts and margarine. Pour into greased 9 x 5 x 3 inch (22 x 12.5 x 7.5 cm) loaf pan. Let stand for 20 minutes. Bake in 350°F (175°C) oven for 1 hour. Cool in pan for 10 minutes. Remove from pan to rack to cool completely. Cuts into 18 slices.

1 slice: 157 Calories; 5.2 g Total Fat; 227 mg Sodium; 2 g Protein; 27 g Carbohydrate; 1 g Dietary Fiber

IRISH WHEAT BREAD

Good flavor to this dense loaf.

Whole wheat flour	3½ cups	875 mL
All-purpose	3 cups	750 mL
Baking soda	1 tsp.	5 mL
Salt	1 tsp.	5 mL
Sour milk (2½ tbsp., 37 mL vinegar, plus milk to make)	2½ cups	625 mL

Measure first 4 ingredients into large bowl. Stir together. Make a well in center.

Pour milk into well in flour mixture. Mix into ball. Knead on lightly floured surface until smooth. Shape into round loaf. Place in greased 8 inch (20 cm) round casserole dish. Bake in 350°F (175°C) oven for about 45 minutes. Cuts into 12 wedges.

1 wedge: 267 Calories; 1.6 g Total Fat; 368 mg Sodium; 10 g Protein; 55 g Carbohydrate; 6 g Dietary Fiber

BEER BREAD

Easy and fast. A delight to toast.

Whole wheat flour	3 cups	750 mL
Baking powder	1 tsp.	5 mL
Baking soda	½ tsp.	2 mL
Salt	½ tsp.	2 mL
Cooking (or fancy) molasses	2 tbsp.	30 mL
Beer, room temperature	12 oz.	355 mL
Hard margarine (or butter), softened, for brushing top	1 tsp.	5 mL

Mix flour, baking powder, baking soda and salt in large bowl.

Add molasses and beer. Stir just to moisten. Dough will be sticky. Turn out onto floured surface. Knead for 1 minute. Put into greased 8 inch (20 cm) round cake pan. Cut lines with sharp knife ½ inch (12 mm) deep, marking 6 to 12 wedges. Bake in 325°F (160°C) oven for 40 to 50 minutes until bread pulls away from side of pan. Remove from pan to rack to cool.

Brush warm top with margarine. Cuts into 12 wedges.

1 wedge: 133 Calories; 0.9 g Total Fat; 179 mg Sodium; 4 g Protein; 26 g Carbohydrate; 4 g Dietary Fiber

APPLE LOAF

A good moist loaf with mild cinnamon and apple flavor.

Large eggs	2	2
Granulated sugar	1 cup	250 mL
Cooking oil	½ cup	125 mL
Vanilla	½ tsp.	2 mL
Peeled and grated cooking apple (such as McIntosh)	2 cups	500 mL
All-purpose flour	2 cups	500 mL
Baking soda	1 tsp.	5 mL
Salt	½ tsp.	2 mL
Raisins	1 cup	250 mL
Chopped walnuts	½ cup	125 mL
Granulated sugar	4 tsp.	20 mL
Ground cinnamon	½ tsp.	2 mL

Beat eggs together in medium bowl until frothy. Beat in first amount of sugar, cooking oil and vanilla. Mix in apple.

Stir flour, baking soda and salt together in small bowl. Add to egg mixture. Mix well. Stir in raisins and walnuts. Scrape into 9 x 5 x 3 inch (22 x 12.5 x 7.5 cm) loaf pan.

Stir second amount of sugar and cinnamon together in small cup. Sprinkle over top. Bake in 350°F (175°C) oven for about 1 hour until wooden pick inserted near center comes out clean. Cuts into 18 slices.

1 slice: 224 Calories; 9.5 g Total Fat; 160 mg Sodium; 3 g Protein; 33 g Carbohydrate; 1 g Dietary Fiber

PUMPERNICKEL

Dark in color, coarse in texture, good in flavor.

Sunny Boy cereal	2 cups	500 mL
All-purpose flour	1 cup	250 mL
Baking powder	1 tsp.	5 mL
Baking soda	1 tsp.	5 mL
Salt	1 tsp.	5 mL
Warm water	2 cups	500 mL
Cooking (or fancy) molasses	¼ cup	60 mL

Combine first 5 ingredients in medium bowl. Stir. Make a well in center.

Stir water and molasses together in small bowl. Pour into well in flour mixture. Stir just to moisten. Batter will be quite runny. Turn into greased 9 x 5 x 3 inch (22 x 12.5 x 7.5 cm) loaf pan. Cover with foil. Bake in 300°F (150°C) oven for about 2 hours. Cool in pan for 10 minutes. Remove from pan to rack to cool completely. Cuts into 16 slices.

1 slice: 115 Calories; 0.6 g Total Fat; 263 mg Sodium; 4 g Protein; 24 g Carbohydrate; 3 g Dietary Fiber

STRAWBERRY BANANA LOAF

A winning combination.

Large eggs	2	2
Cooking oil	¼ cup	60 mL
Granulated sugar	1 cup	250 mL
Mashed fresh strawberry	½ cup	125 mL
Mashed ripe banana (about 2 small)	½ cup	125 mL
All-purpose flour	1¾ cups	425 mL
Rolled oats (not instant)	½ cup	125 mL
Baking powder	2 tsp.	10 mL
Baking soda	½ tsp.	2 mL
Salt	½ tsp.	2 mL

Beat eggs together in large bowl until frothy. Stir in cooking oil, sugar, strawberry and banana.

Combine flour, rolled oats, baking powder, baking soda and salt in small bowl. Stir to distribute evenly. Add to egg mixture. Stir just to moisten. Spoon into greased 9 x 5 x 3 inch (22 x 12.5 x 7.5 cm) loaf pan. Bake in 350°F (175°C) oven for about 1 hour until wooden pick inserted in center comes out clean. Cool in pan for 10 minutes. Remove from pan to rack to cool completely. Wrap and chill for 1 day. Cuts into 18 slices.

1 slice: 146 Calories; 4.1 g Total Fat; 123 mg Sodium; 3 g Protein; 25 g Carbohydrate; 1 g Dietary Fiber

CHOCO BANANA LOAF

A tasty combination of favorite flavors. This slices more easily when it's a day old.

Hard margarine (or butter), softened	½ cup	125 mL
Granulated sugar	1 cup	250 mL
Large eggs	2	2
Vanilla	1 tsp.	5 mL
Mashed ripe banana (about 3 medium)	1 cup	250 mL
Milk	¼ cup	60 mL
All-purpose flour	1½ cups	375mL
Cocoa	¼ cup	60 mL
Baking powder	1½ tsp.	7 mL
Baking soda	½ tsp.	2 mL
Salt	¼ tsp.	1 mL
Chopped walnuts	½ cup	125 mL

Combine margarine, sugar, eggs and vanilla in medium bowl. Beat on medium, just to moisten.

Add banana and milk to batter. Beat on low to blend in.

Add next 5 ingredients. Beat on low until flour mixture is just moistened.

Stir in walnuts. Turn batter into greased 9 x 5 x 3 inch (22 x 12.5 x 7.5 cm) loaf pan. Bake on center rack in 350°F (175°C) oven for 50 to 60 minutes until wooden pick inserted near center comes out clean. Cool in pan for 15 minutes. Remove from pan to rack to cool completely. Cuts into 18 slices.

1 slice: *188 Calories; 8.6 g Total Fat; 151 mg Sodium; 3 g Protein; 26 g Carbohydrate; 1 g Dietary Fiber*

Pictured on page 71.

1. Raspberry Cream Muffins, page 79
2. Cheesy Apple Muffins, page 82
3. Cinnamon Coconut Loaf, page 38
4. Cranberry Orange Loaf, page 38
5. Raisin Orange Biscuits, page 12
6. Confetti Biscuits, page 8
7. Blueberry Streusel Cake, page 22

Props Courtesy Of: Le Gnome;
The Bay

CHEESY BEER BREAD

Serve warm, then toast leftovers. Looks great.

All-purpose flour	2¾ cups	675 mL
Baking powder	4 tsp.	20 mL
Granulated sugar	1 tbsp.	15 mL
Salt	½ tsp.	2 mL
Dry mustard	¼ tsp.	1 mL
Finely grated sharp Cheddar cheese	1 cup	250 mL
Beer, room temperature	12 oz.	355 mL
TOPPING		
Finely grated sharp Cheddar cheese	¼ cup	60 mL
Sesame seed	1 tbsp.	15 mL

Stir first 6 ingredients together in medium bowl.

Add beer. Stir just to moisten. Turn into greased 9 x 5 x 3 inch (22 x 12.5 x 7.5 cm) loaf pan.

Topping: Sprinkle with cheese and sesame seed. Bake in 350°F (175°C) oven for about 50 minutes. Serve warm. Cuts into 18 slices.

1 slice: 123 Calories; 3.2 g Total Fat; 132 mg Sodium; 4 g Protein; 17 g Carbohydrate; 1 g Dietary Fiber

ZUCCHINI LOAF

A large tender loaf.

Large eggs	2	2
Cooking oil	½ cup	125 mL
Granulated sugar	1 cup	250 mL
Grated zucchini, with peel	1 cup	250 mL
Vanilla	1 tsp.	5 mL
All-purpose flour	2 cups	500 mL
Baking powder	1 tsp.	5 mL
Baking soda	1 tsp.	5 mL
Salt	½ tsp.	2 mL
Ground cinnamon	1 tsp.	5 mL

Beat eggs together in medium bowl until frothy. Beat in cooking oil and sugar. Add zucchini. Stir in vanilla.

Combine remaining 5 ingredients in small bowl. Stir together well. Pour into zucchini mixture. Stir just to moisten. Pour into greased 9 x 5 x 3 inch (22 x 12.5 x 7.5 cm) loaf pan. Bake in 350°F (175°C) oven for 50 to 60 minutes until wooden pick inserted in center comes out clean. Cool in pan for 10 minutes. Remove from pan to rack to cool completely. Cuts into 18 slices.

1 slice: 167 Calories; 7.1 g Total Fat; 160 mg Sodium; 2 g Protein; 24 g Carbohydrate; 1 g Dietary Fiber

PINEAPPLE NUT LOAF

Not just a bran loaf—it's healthy and tastes great.

Cooking oil	¼ cup	60 mL
Brown sugar, packed	¾ cup	175 mL
Large egg	1	1
Vanilla	1 tsp.	5 mL
Canned crushed pineapple, with juice	14 oz.	398 mL
All-purpose flour	2¼ cups	560 mL
Baking powder	1 tbsp.	15 mL
Baking soda	½ tsp.	2 mL
Salt	½ tsp.	2 mL
Natural bran	1 cup	250 mL
Chopped walnuts	½ cup	125 mL

Mix cooking oil, brown sugar and egg in large bowl.

Stir in vanilla and pineapple.

Add remaining 6 ingredients. Stir just to moisten. Turn into greased 9 x 5 x 3 inch (22 x 12.5 x 7.5 cm) loaf pan. Bake in 350°F (175°C) oven for about 1 hour until wooden pick inserted in center comes out clean. Cool in pan for 10 minutes. Remove from pan to rack to cool completely. Cuts into 18 slices.

1 slice: 176 Calories; 6.1 g Total Fat; 124 mg Sodium; 3 g Protein; 29 g Carbohydrate; 2 g Dietary Fiber

ORANGE GUMDROP LOAF

Nice and moist. Lots of orange throughout. Freeze for up to two months.

Orange gumdrop slices, cut up	⅓ lb.	150 g
Chopped dates	¾ cup	175 mL
All-purpose flour	⅛ cup	30 mL
Hard margarine (or butter), softened	½ cup	125 mL
Granulated sugar	¾ cup	175 mL
Large eggs	2	2
All-purpose flour	1¾ cups	425 mL
Fine coconut	⅔ cup	150 mL
Baking soda	½ tsp.	2 mL
Chopped pecans	½ cup	125 mL
Salt	¼ tsp.	1 mL
Prepared orange juice	½ cup	125 mL

Toss first 3 ingredients together in small bowl. Set aside.

Cream margarine and sugar together in large bowl. Beat in eggs, 1 at a time.

Stir next 5 ingredients together in medium bowl. Add to egg mixture. Stir.

Stir in orange juice, then fruit mixture. Pour into greased 9 x 5 x 3 inch (22 x 12.5 x 7.5 cm) loaf pan. Bake in 350°F (175°C) oven for about 1¼ hours until wooden pick inserted in center comes out clean. Cool in pan for 10 minutes. Remove from pan to rack to cool completely. Cuts into 18 slices.

1 slice: 237 Calories; 10.8 g Total Fat; 151 mg Sodium; 3 g Protein; 34 g Carbohydrate; 1 g Dietary Fiber

APRICOT CHEESE LOAF

A showy loaf. A bit tart.

Boiling water	1 cup	250 mL
Chopped dried apricot	1 cup	250 mL
Hard margarine (or butter), softened	3 tbsp.	50 mL
Cream cheese, softened	4 oz.	125 g
Granulated sugar	1 cup	250 mL
Large eggs	2	2
All-purpose flour	2 cups	500 mL
Baking powder	2 tsp.	10 mL
Baking soda	½ tsp.	2 mL
Salt	½ tsp.	2 mL
Chopped dates	1 cup	250 mL

Pour boiling water over apricot in small bowl. Cool.

Cream margarine, cream cheese and sugar together in large bowl. Beat in eggs, 1 at a time, until mixture is smooth. Stir in water and cooled apricot.

Combine flour, baking powder, baking soda, salt and dates in small bowl. Mix well. Pour into batter and stir just to moisten. Turn into greased 9 x 5 x 3 inch (22 x 12.5 x 7.5 cm) loaf pan. Bake in 350°F (175°C) oven for 1 hour. Cover with foil. Bake for 10 minutes until wooden pick inserted in center comes out clean. Cool in pan for 10 minutes. Remove from pan to rack to cool completely. Cuts into 18 slices.

1 slice: 191 Calories; 5.2 g Total Fat; 167 mg Sodium; 3 g Protein; 34 g Carbohydrate; 2 g Dietary Fiber

Pictured on page 71.

CRANBERRY ORANGE LOAF

An excellent flavor choice. This loaf tastes even better the next day.

Hard margarine (or butter), softened	¼ cup	60 mL
Granulated sugar	1 cup	250 mL
Large egg	1	1
Juice of 1 orange, plus water to make	¾ cup	175 mL
All-purpose flour	2 cups	500 mL
Baking powder	1½ tsp.	7 mL
Baking soda	½ tsp.	2 mL
Salt	½ tsp.	2 mL
Grated peel of 1 orange		
Whole cranberries (fresh or frozen)	1½ cups	375 mL
Chopped pecans (or walnuts)	½ cup	125 mL

Combine margarine, sugar and egg in medium bowl. Beat together until smooth. Stir in orange juice.

Measure flour, baking powder, baking soda and salt into small bowl. Stir in orange peel, cranberries and pecans. Add to batter, stirring just to moisten. Scrape into greased 9 x 5 x 3 inch (22 x 12.5 x 7.5 cm) loaf pan. Bake in 350°F (175°C) oven for 1 hour until wooden pick inserted near center comes out clean. Cool in pan for 10 minutes. Remove from pan to rack to cool completely. Cuts into 18 slices.

1 slice: 158 Calories; 5.5 g Total Fat; 151 mg Sodium; 2 g Protein; 25 g Carbohydrate; 1 g Dietary Fiber

Pictured on page 35.

Variation: Add ½ cup (125 mL) chopped green cherries. Chop cranberries or leave whole.

CINNAMON COCONUT LOAF

Scrumptious with a pretty swirled effect when sliced.

Large eggs	2	2
Cooking oil	¼ cup	60 mL
Granulated sugar	1 cup	250 mL
Sour cream	1 cup	250 mL
All-purpose flour	1½ cups	375 mL
Baking powder	1½ tsp.	7 mL
Baking soda	1 tsp.	5 mL
Salt	¼ tsp.	1 mL
Medium coconut	½ cup	125 mL
Brown sugar, packed	¼ cup	60 mL
Ground cinnamon	2 tsp.	10 mL

Beat eggs together in large bowl until frothy. Beat in cooking oil and sugar. Blend in sour cream.

Measure flour, baking powder, baking soda and salt into small bowl. Mix well. Add to egg mixture. Stir just to moisten.

Stir coconut, brown sugar and cinnamon together in small bowl. Put ½ of batter into bottom of greased 9 x 5 x 3 inch (22 x 12.5 x 7.5 cm) loaf pan. Sprinkle ½ of cinnamon mixture over top. Spread second ½ of batter over by putting dabs here and there. Sprinkle second ½ of cinnamon mixture over top. Cut through batter with knife to give swirled, marbled effect. Bake in 350°F (175°C) oven for 1 hour. Cool in pan for 10 minutes. Remove from pan to rack to cool completely. Cuts into 18 slices.

1 slice: 173 Calories; 7.5 g Total Fat; 130 mg Sodium; 2 g Protein; 25 g Carbohydrate; 1 g Dietary Fiber

Pictured on page 35.

IRISH SODA BREAD

A quick version of this well-known bread. This may also be baked in a casserole or on a baking sheet.

All-purpose flour	4 cups	1 L
Granulated sugar	2 tbsp.	30 mL
Baking powder	1 tbsp.	15 mL
Baking soda	1 tsp.	5 mL
Salt	1 tsp.	5 mL
Hard margarine (or butter)	6 tbsp.	100 mL
Buttermilk (fresh or reconstituted from powder)	2 cups	500 mL

Combine flour, sugar, baking powder, baking soda and salt in large bowl. Stir thoroughly. Cut in margarine until mixture is crumbly.

Add buttermilk. Stir just to moisten. Turn out onto lightly floured surface. Knead 8 to 10 times. Put into greased 9 x 5 x 3 inch (22 x 12.5 x 7.5 cm) loaf pan. Bake in 350°F (175°C) oven for 1 hour until wooden pick inserted in center comes out clean. Cuts into 18 slices.

1 slice: 160 Calories; 4.5 g Total Fat; 306 mg Sodium; 4 g Protein; 25 g Carbohydrate; 1 g Dietary Fiber

Variation: Add 1 cup (250 mL) currants or raisins.

JOHNNY CAKE

Double flavor. Corn and corn. Good eating corn bread.

Yellow or white cornmeal	1 cup	250 mL
Baking powder	1 tsp.	5 mL
Baking soda	½ tsp.	2 mL
Salt	½ tsp.	2 mL
Large eggs	2	2
Canned cream-style corn	1 cup	250 mL
Cooking oil	¼ cup	60 mL
Sour cream	1 cup	250 mL

Stir cornmeal, baking powder, baking soda and salt together in medium bowl.

Add eggs. Stir together well. Stir in corn, cooking oil and sour cream. Pour into greased 8 x 8 inch (20 x 20 cm) pan. Bake in 400°F (205°C) oven for 25 minutes until browned. Cuts into 9 pieces.

1 piece: 196 Calories; 11.7 g Total Fat; 340 mg Sodium; 4 g Protein; 19 g Carbohydrate; 1 g Dietary Fiber

EGGNOG BREAD

Eggnog flavor comes through nicely.

Granulated sugar	1 cup	250 mL
Large egg	1	1
Hard margarine (or butter), melted	¼ cup	60 mL
Commercial eggnog	1½ cups	375 mL
All-purpose flour	3 cups	750 mL
Baking powder	1 tbsp.	15 mL
Salt	1 tsp.	5 mL
Ground cinnamon	½ tsp.	2 mL
Ground nutmeg	½ tsp.	2 mL
Chopped pecans (or walnuts)	⅔ cup	150 mL
Cut glazed mixed fruit	1 cup	250 mL

Beat sugar and egg together in large bowl. Beat in margarine. Add eggnog. Mix well.

Sift flour, baking powder, salt, cinnamon and nutmeg over eggnog mixture. Stir just to moisten.

Mix in pecans and fruit. Turn into greased 9 x 5 x 3 inch (22 x 12.5 x 7.5 cm) loaf pan. Bake in 350°F (175°C) oven for about 1 hour until wooden pick inserted in center comes out clean. Cool in pan for 20 minutes. Remove from pan to rack to cool completely. Cuts into 18 slices.

1 slice: 250 Calories; 7.8 g Total Fat; 206 mg Sodium; 4 g Protein; 42 g Carbohydrate; 1 g Dietary Fiber

PRUNE LOAF

A nice mild taste of spices. Firm but moist texture. Freezes well.

Hard margarine (or butter), softened	½ cup	125 mL
Granulated sugar	1 cup	250 mL
Large eggs	2	2
Puréed prunes (baby food)	½ cup	125 mL
All-purpose flour	1½ cups	375 mL
Baking soda	1 tsp.	5 mL
Salt	½ tsp.	2 mL
Ground cinnamon	½ tsp.	2 mL
Ground nutmeg	¼ tsp.	1 mL
Ground cloves	¼ tsp.	1 mL
Finely chopped pitted dried prunes	1 cup	250 mL
Chopped pecans (or walnuts)	½ cup	125 mL

Cream margarine and sugar together in medium bowl. Beat in eggs, 1 at a time. Add prunes. Beat together to make smooth mixture.

Stir next 6 ingredients together in small bowl. Add to batter. Stir just to moisten.

Mix in prunes and pecans. Turn into greased 9 x 5 x 3 inch (22 x 12.5 x 7.5 cm) loaf pan. Bake in 350°F (175°C) oven for about 1 hour until wooden pick inserted in center comes out clean. Cool in pan for 10 minutes. Remove from pan to rack to cool completely. Cuts into 18 slices.

1 slice: 190 Calories; 8.5 g Total Fat; 224 mg Sodium; 2 g Protein; 27 g Carbohydrate; 1 g Dietary Fiber

GUMDROP LOAF

This bursts with color. Youngsters love it.

Hard margarine (or butter), softened	½ cup	125 mL
Granulated sugar	1 cup	250 mL
Large eggs	2	2
Vanilla	1 tsp.	5 mL
All-purpose flour	2¼ cups	560 mL
Baking powder	2 tsp.	10 mL
Salt	¼ tsp.	1 mL
Milk	1 cup	250 mL
Regular gumdrops (or baking gums), not black, chopped	1 lb.	454 g
Raisins	1 cup	250 mL

Cream margarine and sugar together well in large bowl. Beat in eggs, 1 at a time. Add vanilla.

Stir flour, baking powder and salt together in small bowl.

Add milk to egg mixture in 2 parts, alternately with flour mixture in 3 parts, beginning and ending with flour mixture.

Stir in gumdrops and raisins. Turn into greased 9 x 5 x 3 inch (22 x 12.5 x 7.5 cm) loaf pan. Bake in 300°F (150°C) oven for about 2 hours until wooden pick inserted in center comes out clean. Cool in pan for 20 minutes. Remove from pan to rack to cool completely. Cuts into 18 slices.

1 slice: 291 Calories; 6.5 g Total Fat; 129 mg Sodium; 3 g Protein; 56 g Carbohydrate; 1 g Dietary Fiber

CHOCOLATE MOCHA LOAF

This loaf has a rippled top like no other. A sprinkling of chocolate chips does the trick.

Hard margarine (or butter), softened	¼ cup	60 mL
Granulated sugar	1 cup	250 mL
Large eggs	2	2
Vanilla	1 tsp.	5 mL
Milk	1 cup	250 mL
Instant coffee granules (optional)	1 tbsp.	15 mL
All-purpose flour	2 cups	500 mL
Cocoa	½ cup	125 mL
Baking powder	1 tbsp.	15 mL
Salt	¾ tsp.	4 mL
Semisweet chocolate chips	½ cup	125 mL

Cream margarine and sugar together in medium bowl. Beat in eggs, 1 at a time. Stir in vanilla, milk and coffee granules.

Stir next 4 ingredients together in small bowl. Add to egg mixture. Stir just to moisten. Turn into greased 9 × 5 × 3 inch (22 × 12.5 × 7.5 cm) loaf pan.

Sprinkle with chocolate chips. Bake in 350°F (175°C) oven for about 1 hour until wooden pick inserted in center comes out clean. Cool in pan for 10 minutes. Remove from pan to rack to cool completely. Cuts into 18 slices.

1 slice: 154 Calories; 4.5 g Total Fat; 163 mg Sodium; 3 g Protein; 27 g Carbohydrate; 2 g Dietary Fiber

LUXURY LOAF

Try this for a smooth textured, different loaf.

Hard margarine (or butter), softened	1 cup	250 mL
Granulated sugar	1 cup	250 mL
Large eggs	5	5
Vanilla	1 tsp.	5 mL
Grated peel of 1 orange		
Prepared orange juice	¼ cup	60 mL
All-purpose flour	2 cups	500 mL
Baking powder	1 tsp.	5 mL
Salt	½ tsp.	2 mL
Ground nutmeg	¼ tsp.	1 mL
Semisweet chocolate baking squares, grated	4 x 1 oz.	4 × 28 g
Chopped nuts	⅓ cup	75 mL

Cream margarine and sugar together in medium bowl until fluffy. Add eggs, 1 at a time, beating well after each addition. Stir in vanilla, orange peel and orange juice.

Combine flour, baking powder, salt and nutmeg in small bowl. Stir in chocolate and nuts. Add to egg mixture. Stir just to moisten. Spoon into greased 9 × 5 × 3 inch (22 × 12.5 × 7.5 cm) loaf pan. Bake in 325°F (160°C) oven for 1¼ hours until wooden pick inserted in center comes out clean. Cool in pan for 10 minutes. Remove from pan to rack to cool completely. Cuts into 18 slices.

1 slice: 267 Calories; 16.2 g Total Fat; 223 mg Sodium; 4 g Protein; 28 g Carbohydrate; 1 g Dietary Fiber

MARMALADE LOAF

Although the fruit is optional, it adds to both the looks and flavor.

Large eggs	2	2
Granulated sugar	¾ cup	175 mL
Hard margarine (or butter), melted	¼ cup	60 mL
Milk	¾ cup	175 mL
Orange marmalade	½ cup	125 mL
White vinegar	2 tbsp.	30 mL
All-purpose flour	2½ cups	625 mL
Baking powder	1 tsp.	5 mL
Baking soda	1 tsp.	5 mL
Salt	1 tsp.	5 mL
Grated peel of ½ lemon		
Grated peel of ½ orange		
Cut glazed mixed fruit (optional)	1 cup	250 mL
Dark brown sugar, packed	2 tbsp.	30 mL

Beat eggs, sugar and margarine together in large bowl. Stir in milk, marmalade and vinegar.

Combine remaining 8 ingredients in medium bowl. Stir well to distribute fruit. Pour all at once into batter. Stir just to moisten. Scrape into greased 9 x 5 x 3 inch (22 x 12.5 x 7.5 cm) loaf pan. Sprinkle brown sugar over top. Bake in 350°F (175°C) oven for 1 hour until wooden pick inserted in center comes out clean. Cool in pan for 10 minutes. Remove from pan to rack to cool completely. Cuts into 18 slices.

1 slice: 167 Calories; 3.4 g Total Fat; 272 mg Sodium; 3 g Protein; 32 g Carbohydrate; 1 g Dietary Fiber

Pictured on page 53 and on back cover.

CHOCOLATE DATE LOAF

A delicious tea bread. Serve with a spread. This loaf cuts better the second day.

Chopped dates	1 cup	250 mL
Boiling water	¾ cup	175 mL
Baking soda	1 tsp.	5 mL
Large egg, fork-beaten	1	1
Granulated sugar	½ cup	125 mL
Salt	¾ tsp.	4 mL
Vanilla	1 tsp.	5 mL
Semisweet chocolate chips, melted	¾ cup	175 mL
Hard margarine (or butter), melted	¼ cup	60 mL
All-purpose flour	1¾ cups	425 mL
Baking powder	1 tsp.	5 mL
Chopped walnuts	½ cup	125 mL

Combine dates, boiling water and baking soda in small bowl. Stir to cool.

Beat egg, sugar, salt and vanilla together in large bowl.

Melt chocolate chips and margarine in small saucepan on low, stirring continually. Mix into egg batter. Stir in date mixture.

Combine flour, baking powder and walnuts in small bowl. Stir well. Add to batter. Stir to mix. Scrape into greased 9 x 5 x 3 inch (22 x 12.5 x 7.5 cm) loaf pan. Let stand for 20 minutes. Bake in 350°F (175°C) oven for 1 hour until wooden pick inserted in center comes out clean. Cool in pan for 10 minutes. Remove from pan to rack to cool completely. Cuts into 18 slices.

1 slice: 176 Calories; 7.4 g Total Fat; 150 mg Sodium; 3 g Protein; 26 g Carbohydrate; 2 g Dietary Fiber

CHOCOLATE CHIP DATE LOAF

Dark and delicious with a fine texture. A large loaf. So good!

Chopped dates	1 cup	250 mL
Baking soda	1 tsp.	5 mL
Boiling water	1 cup	250 mL
Vanilla	1 tsp.	5 mL
Hard margarine (or butter), softened	¾ cup	175 mL
Granulated sugar	1 cup	250 mL
Large eggs	2	2
All-purpose flour	2 cups	500 mL
Cocoa	½ cup	125 mL
Baking soda	1 tsp.	5 mL
Salt	½ tsp.	2 mL
Semisweet chocolate chips	½ cup	125 mL

Combine dates, first amount of baking soda, boiling water and vanilla in small bowl. Stir. Set aside to cool slightly.

Cream margarine and sugar together in large bowl. Add eggs, 1 at a time, beating until smooth. Add date mixture. Stir.

Measure flour, cocoa, second amount of baking soda, salt and chocolate chips into small bowl. Stir to mix well. Add to date mixture. Stir just to moisten. Spoon into greased 9 x 5 x 3 inch (22 x 12.5 x 7.5 cm) loaf pan. Bake in 350°F (175°C) oven for 1 hour until wooden pick inserted in center comes out clean. Cool in pan for 10 minutes. Remove from pan to rack to cool completely. Cuts into 18 slices.

1 slice: 230 Calories; 10.6 g Total Fat; 332 mg Sodium; 3 g Protein; 33 g Carbohydrate; 3 g Dietary Fiber

SAVORY ONION BREAD

Looks great. Tastes great. Goes well with green salads.

All-purpose flour	1½ cups	375 mL
Baking powder	1 tbsp.	15 mL
Salt	1 tsp.	5 mL
Hard margarine (or butter)	2 tbsp.	30 mL
Grated sharp Cheddar cheese	½ cup	125 mL
Finely chopped onion	½ cup	125 mL
Hard margarine (or butter)	1 tbsp.	15 mL
Large egg, fork-beaten	1	1
Milk	½ cup	125 mL
Grated sharp Cheddar cheese	½ cup	125 mL

Combine flour, baking powder and salt in large bowl. Cut in first amount of margarine until mixture is crumbly. Stir in cheese. Make a well in center.

Sauté onion in second amount of margarine in small frying pan until clear and golden. Set aside.

Beat egg with spoon in small bowl. Stir in milk. Add onion. Pour into well in flour mixture. Stir just to moisten and form soft dough. Pat into greased 8 inch (20 cm) round cake or 8 x 8 inch (20 x 20 cm) pan.

Sprinkle cheese over top. Bake in 400°F (205°C) oven for 25 minutes. Cuts into 9 pieces.

1 piece: 188 Calories; 9.3 g Total Fat; 450 mg Sodium; 7 g Protein; 19 g Carbohydrate; 1 g Dietary Fiber

Pictured on page 17.

LEMON CHEESE LOAF

Flavor is tangy. Texture is moist. Cream cheese cubes show evenly throughout.

Hard margarine (or butter), softened	½ cup	125 mL
Granulated sugar	1¼ cups	300 mL
Large eggs	2	2
Milk	¾ cup	175 mL
Grated peel of 1 lemon		
All-purpose flour	2 cups	500 mL
Baking powder	2 tsp.	10 mL
Salt	¾ tsp.	4 mL
Cream cheese, cut into ¼ inch (6 mm) cubes	8 oz.	250 g
Chopped walnuts	½ cup	125 mL
TOPPING		
Juice of 1 lemon		
Granulated sugar	¼ cup	60 mL

Cream margarine and sugar together in large bowl. Beat in eggs, 1 at a time. Mix in milk and lemon peel.

Stir flour, baking powder and salt together in small bowl. Add to batter. Stir just to moisten.

Fold in cream cheese and walnuts. Turn into greased 9 x 5 x 3 inch (22 x 12.5 x 7.5 cm) loaf pan. Bake in 350°F (175°C) oven for about 1¼ hours until wooden pick inserted in center comes out clean.

Topping: Stir lemon juice and sugar together in small saucepan. Heat and stir until sugar is dissolved. Poke 8 or 10 holes in top of loaf with wooden pick. Spoon syrup over loaf. Cool in pan for 10 minutes. Remove from pan to rack to cool completely. Cuts into 18 slices.

1 slice: 257 Calories; 13.4 g Total Fat; 233 mg Sodium; 4 g Protein; 31 g Carbohydrate; 1 g Dietary Fiber

CRANBERRY CORN BREAD

So quick to make. Savory corn bread flavor with the sweetness of cranberry. Freezes well.

Hard margarine (or butter), melted	6 tbsp.	100 mL
Brown sugar, packed	½ cup	125 mL
Large egg	1	1
Buttermilk (fresh or reconstituted from powder)	1 cup	250 mL
Coarsely chopped cranberries (fresh or frozen)	1 cup	250 mL
Yellow cornmeal	1 cup	250 mL
All-purpose flour	1 cup	250 mL
Baking powder	1 tbsp.	15 mL
Salt	½ tsp.	2 mL
Chopped walnuts	⅔ cup	150 mL

Beat margarine, brown sugar and egg together in medium bowl. Mix in buttermilk. Add cranberries. Stir together.

Add cornmeal, flour, baking powder and salt. Stir just to moisten. Turn into greased 9 x 9 inch (22 x 22 cm) pan.

Sprinkle with walnuts. Bake in 400°F (205°C) oven for about 25 minutes until wooden pick inserted in center comes out clean. Best served warm. Cuts into 16 pieces.

1 piece: 178 Calories; 8.1 g Total Fat; 159 mg Sodium; 3 g Protein; 23 g Carbohydrate; 1 g Dietary Fiber

Tea loaves are often better in texture and taste the day after baking. Cool completely, then wrap airtight and store in the refrigerator for up to three days.

BLUEBERRY LOAF

Delicious blueberries throughout. Make ahead with the glaze, and freeze.

Hard margarine (or butter), softened	½ cup	125 mL
Granulated sugar	1 cup	250 mL
Large eggs	2	2
Buttermilk	⅔ cup	150 mL
Grated peel of 1 medium lemon		
All-purpose flour	2 cups	500 mL
Baking powder	2 tsp.	10 mL
Salt	½ tsp.	2 mL
Blueberries (fresh or frozen)	1½ cups	375 mL
All-purpose flour	1 tbsp.	15 mL
GLAZE		
Lemon juice	3 tbsp.	50 mL
Granulated sugar	¼ cup	60 mL

Cream margarine and sugar together in large bowl. Beat in eggs, 1 at a time. Add buttermilk and lemon peel. Mix.

Measure first amount of flour, baking powder and salt into medium bowl. Stir together well. Add to batter. Stir just to moisten.

Toss blueberries with second amount of flour in small bowl. Add to batter, stirring gently and quickly. Turn into greased 9 x 5 x 3 inch (22 x 12.5 x 7.5 cm) loaf pan. Bake in 350°F (175°C) oven for about 1½ hours until wooden pick inserted in center comes out clean.

Glaze: Stir lemon juice and sugar together in small saucepan until sugar is dissolved. Spoon syrup evenly over top of hot loaf before removing from pan. Cool in pan for 10 minutes. Remove from pan to rack to cool completely. Cuts into 18 slices.

1 slice: 192 Calories; 6.3 g Total Fat; 159 mg Sodium; 3 g Protein; 32 g Carbohydrate; 1 g Dietary Fiber

Pictured on front cover.

PRUNE BREAD

Both orange and prune flavors can be tasted.

Cooking oil	3 tbsp.	50 mL
Granulated sugar	⅔ cup	150 mL
Large egg	1	1
Vanilla	½ tsp.	2 mL
Medium orange, ground	⅔ cup	150 mL
Prepared orange juice	½ cup	125 mL
Stewed pitted prunes, chopped	1 cup	250 mL
All-purpose flour	2 cups	500 mL
Baking powder	2½ tsp.	12 mL
Baking soda	½ tsp.	2 mL
Salt	½ tsp.	2 mL
Chopped walnuts	½ cup	125 mL

Beat cooking oil, sugar and egg together in large bowl until smooth. Stir in vanilla. Add orange. Mix in orange juice and prunes.

Measure flour, baking powder, baking soda, salt and walnuts into small bowl. Stir together well. Add to egg mixture. Stir just to moisten. Turn into greased 9 x 5 x 3 inch (22 x 12.5 x 7.5 cm) loaf pan. Bake in 350°F (175°C) oven for 1 hour until wooden pick inserted in center comes out clean. Cool in pan for 10 minutes. Remove from pan to rack to cool completely. Cuts into 18 slices.

1 slice: 153 Calories; 5.1 g Total Fat; 120 mg Sodium; 3 g Protein; 26 g Carbohydrate; 2 g Dietary Fiber

BRAZIL LOAF

This is a solid nutty loaf with cherries adding the color.

Whole Brazil nuts	3 cups	750 mL
Glazed cherries	2¼ cups	560 mL
Glazed pineapple rings, cubed	4	4
All-purpose flour	1¼ cups	300 mL
Granulated sugar	¾ cup	175 mL
Baking powder	1 tsp.	5 mL
Salt	½ tsp.	2 mL
Large eggs	3	3
Hard margarine (or butter), softened	½ cup	125 mL
Vanilla	1 tsp.	5 mL
Almond flavoring	1 tsp.	5 mL

Place first 3 ingredients in large bowl.

Combine flour, sugar, baking powder and salt in small bowl. Add to fruit. Stir thoroughly to coat.

Beat eggs together in small bowl until frothy. Add margarine, vanilla and almond flavoring. Mix. Pour over fruit mixture. Stir just to moisten. Turn into 9 x 5 x 3 inch (22 x 12.5 x 7.5 cm) loaf pan lined with greased brown paper. Press down. Bake in 300°F (150°C) oven for 1¾ to 2 hours until wooden pick inserted in center comes out clean. Cool in pan for 20 minutes. Remove from pan to rack to cool completely. Discard brown paper. Cuts into 18 slices.

1 slice: 404 Calories; 22.8 g Total Fat; 152 mg Sodium; 6 g Protein; 48 g Carbohydrate; 2 g Dietary Fiber

Pictured on front cover.

APPLE CHERRY BREAD

Excellent cherry and nut flavor with just a hint of almond. Prepare cherries and walnuts in the morning. Freezes well.

Hard margarine (or butter), softened	½ cup	125 mL
Granulated sugar	¾ cup	175 mL
Large eggs	2	2
Almond flavoring	½ tsp.	2 mL
Canned applesauce	1 cup	250 mL
Reserved maraschino cherry juice	2 tbsp.	30 mL
All-purpose flour	2 cups	500 mL
Baking powder	2 tsp.	10 mL
Baking soda	½ tsp.	2 mL
Salt	½ tsp.	2 mL
Chopped walnuts	½ cup	125 mL
Chopped maraschino cherries, blotted dry, juice reserved	¾ cup	175 mL

Cream margarine and sugar together in medium bowl. Beat in eggs, 1 at a time. Mix in almond flavoring.

Add applesauce and cherry juice. Stir.

Stir flour, baking powder, baking soda and salt together in small bowl. Add to applesauce mixture. Stir just to moisten.

Stir in walnuts and cherries. Turn into greased 9 x 5 x 3 inch (22 x 12.5 x 7.5 cm) loaf pan. Bake in 350°F (175°C) oven for about 55 minutes until wooden pick inserted in center comes out clean. Cool in pan for 20 minutes. Remove from pan to rack to cool completely. Cuts into 18 slices.

1 slice: 181 Calories; 8.4 g Total Fat; 187 mg Sodium; 3 g Protein; 24 g Carbohydrate; 1 g Dietary Fiber

CARROT LOAF

Really tasty and spicy.

Cooking oil	½ cup	125 mL
Large eggs	2	2
Granulated sugar	1 cup	250 mL
Finely grated carrot	1 cup	250 mL
All-purpose flour	1¾ cups	425 mL
Baking powder	2 tsp.	10 mL
Baking soda	½ tsp.	2 mL
Ground cinnamon	1 tsp.	5 mL
Ground nutmeg	¾ tsp.	4 mL
Ground cloves	¼ tsp.	1 mL
Ground ginger	¼ tsp.	1 mL
Chopped walnuts	½ cup	125 mL

Beat cooking oil, eggs and sugar together in medium bowl until blended. Stir in carrot.

Combine remaining 8 ingredients in small bowl. Pour into carrot batter. Stir just to moisten. Turn into greased 9 x 5 x 3 inch (22 x 12.5 x 7.5 cm) loaf pan. Bake in 350°F (175°C) oven for about 1 hour until wooden pick inserted in center comes out clean. Cool in pan for 10 minutes. Remove from pan to rack to cool completely. Cuts into 18 slices.

1 slice: 185 Calories; 9.4 g Total Fat; 50 mg Sodium; 3 g Protein; 23 g Carbohydrate; 1 g Dietary Fiber

Pictured on page 71.

GLUTEN-FREE BREAD

Freeze part of the loaf and use as needed.

Cooking oil	⅓ cup	75 mL
Granulated sugar	2 tbsp.	30 mL
Large eggs	2	2
Milk	1 cup	250 mL
Lemon flavoring	½ tsp.	2 mL
Rice (or white or whole wheat) flour	2 cups	500 mL
Potato starch	1 cup	250 mL
Gluten-free baking powder	4 tsp.	20 mL
Salt	½ tsp.	2 mL

Beat cooking oil, sugar and eggs together well in medium bowl. Add milk and lemon flavoring. Mix.

Add remaining 4 ingredients. Beat on lowest speed to moisten. Turn into greased 9 x 5 x 3 inch (22 x 12.5 x 7.5 cm) loaf pan. Bake in 350°F (175°C) oven for 35 to 40 minutes until wooden pick inserted in center comes out clean. Remove from pan to rack to cool. Cuts into 16 slices.

1 slice: 184 Calories; 6 g Total Fat; 109 mg Sodium; 4 g Protein; 29 g Carbohydrate; 1 g Dietary Fiber

TROPICAL LOAF

Incredibly delicious and attractive.

Large eggs	2	2
Granulated sugar	¾ cup	175 mL
Cooking oil	½ cup	125 mL
Mashed ripe banana (about 3)	1 cup	250 mL
Canned crushed pineapple, drained	14 oz.	398 mL
Vanilla	1 tsp.	5 mL
Maraschino cherries, drained and halved	⅔ cup	150 mL
Chopped pecans (or walnuts)	½ cup	125 mL
All-purpose flour	1¾ cups	425 mL
Baking soda	½ tsp.	2 mL
Baking powder	½ tsp.	2 mL
Salt	½ tsp.	2 mL

Beat eggs together in medium bowl until frothy. Beat in sugar. Stir in next 6 ingredients.

Add remaining 4 ingredients. Stir just to moisten. Turn into greased 9 x 5 x 3 inch (22 x 12.5 x 7.5 cm) loaf pan. Bake in 350°F (175°C) oven for 60 to 70 minutes until wooden pick inserted in center comes out clean. Cool in pan for 10 minutes. Remove from pan to rack to cool completely. Cuts into 18 slices.

1 slice: 194 Calories; 9.5 g Total Fat; 122 mg Sodium; 3 g Protein; 26 g Carbohydrate; 1 g Dietary Fiber

CHOCOLATE LOAF

Dark and sweet.

Semisweet chocolate baking squares, cut up	4 × 1 oz.	4 × 28 g
Hard margarine (or butter), softened	½ cup	125 mL
Brown sugar, packed	1 cup	250 mL
Large eggs	2	2
Vanilla	1 tsp.	5 mL
Milk	1 cup	250 mL
All-purpose flour	2 cups	500 mL
Baking powder	1 tsp.	5 mL
Baking soda	½ tsp.	2 mL
Salt	½ tsp.	2 mL
Semisweet chocolate chips	½ cup	125 mL

Melt baking squares in small saucepan on low, stirring often. Remove from heat.

Cream margarine and brown sugar together in medium bowl. Add eggs, 1 at a time, beating well after each addition. Add vanilla and milk. Mix. Beat in chocolate.

Stir flour, baking powder, baking soda and salt together in small bowl. Add to chocolate batter. Stir just to moisten.

Add chocolate chips. Mix. Turn into greased 9 × 5 × 3 inch (22 × 12.5 × 7.5 cm) loaf pan. Bake in 350°F (175°C) oven for about 1 hour until wooden pick inserted in center comes out clean. Cool in pan for 15 minutes. Remove from pan to rack to cool completely. Cuts into 18 slices.

1 slice: 218 Calories; 10 g Total Fat; 198 mg Sodium; 3 g Protein; 31 g Carbohydrate; 1 g Dietary Fiber

HARVEST LOAF

A brown loaf with dark brown dots. Very tasty.

Hard margarine (or butter), softened	½ cup	125 mL
Granulated sugar	1 cup	250 mL
Large eggs	2	2
Canned pumpkin (without spices)	1 cup	250 mL
All-purpose flour	2 cups	500 mL
Baking powder	1½ tsp.	7 mL
Baking soda	½ tsp.	2 mL
Salt	½ tsp.	2 mL
Ground cinnamon	½ tsp.	2 mL
Ground nutmeg	½ tsp.	2 mL
Ground ginger	½ tsp.	2 mL
Semisweet chocolate chips	1 cup	250 mL
Chopped nuts	½ cup	125 mL

Cream margarine and sugar together in large bowl. Beat in eggs, 1 at a time, until smooth. Stir in pumpkin.

Combine remaining 9 ingredients in medium bowl. Mix well. Add to egg mixture. Stir together just to moisten. Spoon into greased 9 × 5 × 3 inch (22 × 12.5 × 7.5 cm) loaf pan. Bake in 350°F (175°C) oven for 1 hour until wooden pick inserted in center comes out clean. Cool in pan for 10 minutes. Remove from pan to rack to cool completely. Cuts into 18 slices.

1 slice: 226 Calories; 11.4 g Total Fat; 188 mg Sodium; 3 g Protein; 30 g Carbohydrate; 1 g Dietary Fiber

For a different shape, bake tea loaves in an 8 x 8 inch (20 x 20 cm) pan and reduce baking time to 25 to 30 minutes. Or, bake in mini-loaf pans (4 mini loaves can be made from the batter of 1 large loaf). Bake for about 20 minutes.

HOLIDAY BANANA LOAF

Double this recipe to have enough for smaller gift loaves.

Hard margarine (or butter), softened	½ cup	125 mL
Granulated sugar	1 cup	250 mL
Large eggs	2	2
Vanilla	1 tsp.	5 mL
All-purpose flour	1¾ cups	425 mL
Baking soda	1 tsp.	5 mL
Baking powder	1 tsp.	5 mL
Salt	½ tsp.	2 mL
Chopped walnuts	¼ cup	60 mL
Fine coconut	½ cup	125 mL
Chopped maraschino cherries	½ cup	125 mL
All-purpose flour	¼ cup	60 mL
Mashed ripe banana (about 3)	1 cup	250 mL

Cream margarine and sugar together in medium bowl. Add eggs, 1 at a time, beating well after each addition. Add vanilla. Stir.

Measure first amount of flour, baking soda, baking powder and salt into small bowl. Stir.

Toss walnuts, coconut and cherries together with second amount of flour in separate small bowl.

Add flour mixture in 4 additions, alternately with banana in 3 additions, beginning and ending with flour mixture. Add fruit mixture. Stir just to moisten. Turn into greased 9 x 5 x 3 inch (22 x 12.5 x 7.5 cm) loaf pan. Bake in 350°F (175°C) oven for 50 to 60 minutes until wooden pick inserted in center comes out clean. Cool in pan for 20 minutes. Remove from pan to rack to cool completely. Cuts into 18 slices.

1 slice: 216 Calories; 9.1 g Total Fat; 225 mg Sodium; 3 g Protein; 32 g Carbohydrate; 1 g Dietary Fiber

RHUBARB BREAD

Rhubarb and orange combine to make a colorful loaf. Tasty.

Finely cut fresh rhubarb	1 cup	250 mL
Granulated sugar	¼ cup	60 mL
Granulated sugar	1 cup	250 mL
Hard margarine (or butter), melted	¼ cup	60 mL
Large egg	1	1
Juice and grated peel of 1 orange		
Milk added to make	1 cup	250 mL
All-purpose flour	3 cups	750 mL
Baking powder	1½ tbsp.	25 mL
Salt	½ tsp.	2 mL

Combine rhubarb and first amount of sugar. Let stand for 15 minutes.

Beat second amount of sugar, margarine and egg together in large bowl. Beat together well.

Put orange juice and grated peel into measuring cup. Add milk to measure 1 cup (250 mL). Stir into egg mixture.

Stir flour, baking powder and salt together. Add to egg mixture. Stir just to moisten. Turn into greased 9 x 5 x 3 inch (22 x 12.5 x 7.5 cm) loaf pan. Bake in 350°F (175°C) oven for about 1 hour until wooden pick inserted in center comes out clean. Cool in pan for 10 minutes. Remove from pan to rack to cool completely. Cuts into 18 slices.

1 slice: 171 Calories; 3.1 g Total Fat; 116 mg Sodium; 3 g Protein; 34 g Carbohydrate; 1 g Dietary Fiber

CHOCOLATE ZUCCHINI LOAF

Make several in the fall when zucchini are more plentiful. Freeze and bring out for Christmas.

Hard margarine (or butter), softened	6 tbsp.	100 mL
Granulated sugar	1 cup	250 mL
Large egg	1	1
Vanilla	1 tsp.	5 mL
Grated zucchini, with peel	1 cup	250 mL
All-purpose flour	1½ cups	375 mL
Cocoa	¼ cup	60 mL
Baking powder	1¼ tsp.	6 mL
Baking soda	¾ tsp.	4 mL
Salt	½ tsp.	2 mL
Ground cinnamon	½ tsp.	2 mL
Milk	¼ cup	60 mL
Chopped walnuts	½ cup	125 mL

Cream margarine and sugar together in medium bowl. Beat in egg. Add vanilla and zucchini. Stir together.

Add next 6 ingredients. Stir just to moisten.

Add milk and walnuts. Stir gently to mix. Turn into greased 9 x 5 x 3 inch (22 x 12.5 x 7.5 cm) loaf pan. Bake in 350°F (175°C) oven for about 1 hour until wooden pick inserted in center comes out clean. Cool in pan for 10 minutes. Remove from pan to rack to cool completely. Cuts into 18 slices.

1 slice: 155 Calories; 6.7 g Total Fat; 186 mg Sodium; 3 g Protein; 22 g Carbohydrate; 1 g Dietary Fiber

BISHOP'S BREAD

Rich looking. Rich tasting.

Large egg	1	1
Granulated sugar	½ cup	125 mL
Cooking oil	¼ cup	60 mL
Vanilla	1 tsp.	5 mL
Sour milk (1 tbsp., 15 mL, white vinegar plus milk to make)	1 cup	250 mL
All-purpose flour	2 cups	500 mL
Baking soda	½ tsp.	2 mL
Salt	½ tsp.	2 mL
Chopped walnuts	½ cup	125 mL
Chopped glazed cherries	½ cup	125 mL
Raisins (or currants)	½ cup	125 mL
Semisweet chocolate chips	½ cup	125 mL

Beat egg in large bowl until frothy. Add sugar, cooking oil and vanilla. Beat to blend. Mix in sour milk.

Measure flour, baking soda and salt into medium bowl. Stir to mix well. Add walnuts, cherries, raisins and chocolate chips. Mix. Add all at once to egg mixture. Stir just to moisten. Spoon into greased 9 x 5 x 3 inch (22 x 12.5 x 7.5 cm) loaf pan. Bake in 350°F (175°C) oven for 1 hour until wooden pick inserted in center comes out clean. Cool in pan for 10 minutes. Remove from pan to rack to cool completely. Cuts into 18 slices.

1 slice: 190 Calories; 7.6 g Total Fat; 126 mg Sodium; 3 g Protein; 29 g Carbohydrate; 1 g Dietary Fiber

STRAWBERRY BREAD

Light cake-like texture. Flecks of red jam throughout.

Hard margarine (or butter), softened	½ cup	125 mL
Granulated sugar	¾ cup	175 mL
Large eggs	2	2
Vanilla	¾ tsp.	4 mL
Lemon juice	¼ tsp.	1 mL
Strawberry jam, stirred	⅓ cup	75 mL
Sour cream	¼ cup	60 mL
All-purpose flour	1½ cups	375 mL
Cream of tartar	½ tsp.	2 mL
Baking soda	¼ tsp.	1 mL

Cream margarine and sugar together in medium bowl. Beat in eggs, 1 at a time, beating well after each addition. Mix in vanilla and lemon juice.

Stir jam and sour cream together in small bowl.

Sift remaining 3 ingredients together. Add flour mixture to egg mixture in 3 parts, alternately with jam mixture in 2 parts, beginning and ending with flour mixture. Stir just to moisten. Turn into greased 8 x 4 x 3 inch (20 x 10 x 7.5 cm) loaf pan. Bake in 350°F (175°C) oven for 55 to 60 minutes until wooden pick inserted in center comes out clean. Cool in pan for 20 minutes. Remove from pan to rack to cool completely. Cuts into 16 slices.

1 slice: 173 Calories; 7.4 g Total Fat; 115 mg Sodium; 2 g Protein; 25 g Carbohydrate; trace Dietary Fiber

BANANA BRAN LOAF

How lucky—this is both good and healthy.

Large eggs	2	2
Mashed ripe banana (about 3 medium)	1 cup	250 mL
Granulated sugar	⅔ cup	150 mL
Cooking oil	⅓ cup	75 mL
Vanilla	1 tsp.	5 mL
All-purpose flour	1 cup	250 mL
Natural bran	1 cup	250 mL
Baking powder	2 tsp.	10 mL
Baking soda	½ tsp.	2 mL
Salt	½ tsp.	2 mL
Chopped walnuts (optional)	½ cup	125 mL

Beat eggs together in large bowl until smooth.

Add banana, sugar, cooking oil and vanilla. Mix well.

Add remaining 6 ingredients. Stir just to moisten. Turn into greased 9 x 5 x 3 inch (22 x 12.5 x 7.5 cm) loaf pan. Bake in 350°F (175°C) oven for 50 to 60 minutes until wooden pick inserted in center comes out clean. Cuts into 18 slices.

1 slice: 124 Calories; 5.1 g Total Fat; 123 mg Sodium; 2 g Protein; 19 g Carbohydrate; 2 g Dietary Fiber

Always test loaves with a wooden pick or cake tester at the minimum time given. Then add time in small amounts until result is as stated in recipe.

BOSTON BROWN BREAD

Bake some beans to complete the meal.

Whole wheat flour	1 cup	250 mL
Cornmeal	1 cup	250 mL
All-purpose flour	1 cup	250 mL
Brown sugar, packed	2 tbsp.	30 mL
Baking powder	1 tsp.	5 mL
Baking soda	1 tsp.	5 mL
Salt	1 tsp.	5 mL
Raisins (optional)	1 cup	250 mL
Water	1¼ cups	300 mL
Cooking (or fancy) molasses	¾ cup	175 mL
Cooking oil	2 tbsp.	30 mL

Combine all 7 dry ingredients in large bowl. Add raisins. Stir to blend thoroughly. Make a well in center.

Stir water and molasses together in small bowl until blended. Add cooking oil. Pour into well in flour mixture. Stir just to moisten. Batter will be lumpy. Fill 2 greased 28 oz. (796 mL) or 3 greased 19 oz. (540 mL) cans ⅔ full. Cover with foil and secure with string. Place cans on rack in pan with boiling water halfway up the sides of cans. Cover pan. Steam for 2 hours. Add more boiling water as needed to keep water halfway up cans. Remove bread from cans. Serve hot or cold. Makes about 3 round loaves, about 8 slices each.

1 slice: *102 Calories; 1.4 g Total Fat; 173 mg Sodium; 2 g Protein; 21 g Carbohydrate; 1 g Dietary Fiber*

Pictured on page 71.

DATE GRAHAM LOAF

This is a dark, good loaf.

Chopped dates	1 cup	250 mL
Boiling water	1 cup	250 mL
Baking soda	1 tsp.	5 mL
Large egg, fork-beaten	1	1
Hard margarine (or butter), melted	2 tbsp.	30 mL
Granulated sugar	¾ cup	175 mL
Vanilla	1 tsp.	5 mL
All-purpose flour	1 cup	250 mL
Graham flour	1 cup	250 mL
Baking powder	2 tsp.	10 mL
Salt	½ tsp.	2 mL
Chopped walnuts (optional)	½ cup	125 mL

Combine dates, boiling water and baking soda in large bowl. Cool slightly.

Beat egg, margarine, sugar and vanilla together in small bowl. Stir into date mixture.

Combine remaining 5 ingredients in medium bowl. Mix well. Stir into batter. Scrape into greased 9 x 5 x 3 inch (22 x 12.5 x 7.5 cm) loaf pan. Bake in 350°F (175°C) oven for 1 hour until wooden pick inserted in center comes out clean. Cool in pan for 10 minutes. Remove from pan to rack to cool completely. Cuts into 18 slices.

1 slice: *124 Calories; 1.7 g Total Fat; 172 mg Sodium; 2 g Protein; 126 g Carbohydrate; 2 g Dietary Fiber*

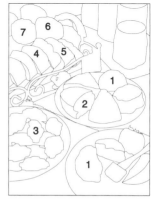

Props Courtesy Of: La Cache; Stokes; The Basket House; The Glasshouse

BANANA LOAF

This is a good gluten-free version.

Large eggs	2	2
Granulated sugar	1/2 cup	125 mL
Cooking oil	1/4 cup	60 mL
Vanilla	1 tsp.	5 mL
Salt	1/2 tsp.	2 mL
Mashed ripe banana (about 3 medium)	1 cup	250 mL
Milk	1/4 cup	60 mL
Brown rice flour	1 1/4 cups	300 mL
Potato starch	1/2 cup	125 mL
Tapioca flour	1/4 cup	60 mL
Cocoa	1 tsp.	5 mL
Gluten-free baking powder	1 tbsp.	15 mL
Baking soda	1/4 tsp.	1 mL

Beat eggs together in medium bowl. Add next 6 ingredients. Beat. Mixture will be curdly.

Add remaining 6 ingredients. Beat to mix. Turn into greased 9 x 5 x 3 inch (22 x 12.5 x 7.5 cm) loaf pan. Bake in 350°F (175°C) oven for about 45 minutes until wooden pick inserted in center comes out clean. Cool in pan for 10 minutes. Remove from pan to rack to cool completely. Cuts into 18 slices.

1 slice: 143 Calories; 4.3 g Total Fat; 109 mg Sodium; 2 g Protein; 25 g Carbohydrate; 1 g Dietary Fiber

CHERRY BRAN LOAF

A cherry almond flavor. A pretty loaf.

Hard margarine (or butter), softened	1/4 cup	60 mL
Granulated sugar	3/4 cup	175 mL
Large egg	1	1
Milk	1 cup	250 mL
Almond flavoring	1/2 tsp.	2 mL
All-purpose flour	2 cups	500 mL
All-bran cereal	1 cup	250 mL
Baking powder	1 tbsp.	15 mL
Salt	1 tsp.	5 mL
Maraschino cherries, drained and chopped	2/3 cup	150 mL
Chopped walnuts (or pecans)	1/2 cup	125 mL

Cream margarine and sugar together in medium bowl. Beat in egg. Add milk and almond flavoring. Stir together.

Add next 4 ingredients. Stir just to moisten.

Add cherries and walnuts. Stir enough to distribute. Turn into greased 9 x 5 x 3 inch (22 x 12.5 x 7.5 cm) loaf pan. Bake in 350°F (175°C) oven for 50 to 60 minutes until wooden pick inserted in center comes out clean. Cool in pan for 10 minutes. Remove from pan to rack to cool completely. Cuts into 18 slices.

1 slice: 161 Calories; 5.7 g Total Fat; 232 mg Sodium; 3 g Protein; 26 g Carbohydrate; 2 g Dietary Fiber

Cream margarine and sugar together more easily by first sprinkling a few drops of water on top.

★★

RAISIN BREAD

Out of bread? This cinnamon flavored bread fills the bill. Good toasted too.

All-purpose flour	3 cups	750 mL
Granulated sugar	½ cup	125 mL
Baking powder	1 tbsp.	15 mL
Baking soda	½ tsp.	2 mL
Salt	1 tsp.	5 mL
Ground cinnamon	¾ tsp.	4 mL
Raisins	1 cup	250 mL
Large egg	1	1
Hard margarine (or butter), melted	¼ cup	60 mL
Milk	1 cup	250 mL

Measure first 7 ingredients into large bowl. Stir thoroughly. Make a well in center.

Beat egg in small bowl until frothy. Mix in margarine and milk. Pour into well in flour mixture. Stir just to moisten. Scrape into greased 9 x 5 x 3 inch (22 x 12.5 x 7.5 cm) loaf pan. Bake in 350°F (175°C) oven for 1 hour. Cool in pan for 10 minutes. Remove from pan to rack to cool completely. Cuts into 18 slices.

1 slice: 162 Calories; 3.2 g Total Fat; 233 mg Sodium; 3 g Protein; 30 g Carbohydrate; 1 g Dietary Fiber

CHEESE LOAF

Moist, delicious and attractive. A good bread substitute. And so simple to make.

All-purpose flour	3 cups	750 mL
Baking powder	4 tsp.	20 mL
Salt	½ tsp.	2 mL
Grated medium or sharp Cheddar cheese	1½ cups	375 mL
Milk	1½ cups	375 mL
Hard margarine (or butter), melted	2 tbsp.	30 mL

Combine flour, baking powder, salt and cheese in large bowl. Stir together thoroughly.

Add milk and margarine. Stir to form soft dough. Put into greased 9 x 5 x 3 inch (22 x 12.5 x 7.5 cm) loaf pan. Bake in 400°F (205°C) oven for 35 to 40 minutes. Cool in pan for 10 minutes. Remove from pan to rack to cool. Cuts into 16 slices.

1 slice: 159 Calories; 5.6 g Total Fat; 187 mg Sodium; 6 g Protein; 21 g Carbohydrate; 1 g Dietary Fiber

TOFFEE LOAF

Sweetened condensed milk gives this favorite loaf its distinctive toffee flavor.

Sweetened condensed milk	11 oz.	300 mL
Water	1 cup	250 mL
Hard margarine (or butter)	1 cup	250 mL
Raisins	1¼ cups	300 mL
Currants	½ cup	125 mL
Chopped dates	1 cup	250 mL
All-purpose flour	2 cups	500 mL
Baking soda	1 tsp.	5 mL
Salt	⅛ tsp.	0.5 mL

Measure condensed milk, water and margarine into large saucepan. Stir together on medium until mixture boils. Simmer for 3 minutes, stirring frequently to prevent sticking. Remove from heat.

Stir in raisins, currants and dates. Let stand until just warm.

Mix flour, baking soda and salt in small bowl. Add to fruit mixture. Turn into greased 9 x 5 x 3 inch (22 x 12.5 x 7.5 cm) loaf pan. Bake in 325°F (160°C) oven for about 2 hours. Cover with foil halfway through baking if top is getting dark. Cool in pan for 5 minutes. Remove from pan to rack to cool completely. Cuts into 18 slices.

1 slice: 287 Calories; 13 g Total Fat; 253 mg Sodium; 4 g Protein; 41 g Carbohydrate; 2 g Dietary Fiber

CHERRY MARASCHINO LOAF

Cherries add color and flavor to this pretty pink loaf.

Hard margarine (or butter), softened	¼ cup	60 mL
Granulated sugar	1 cup	250 mL
Large egg	1	1
Milk	⅔ cup	150 mL
Maraschino cherry juice	⅓ cup	75 mL
Almond flavoring	1 tsp.	5 mL
All-purpose flour	2¼ cups	560 mL
Baking powder	2 tsp.	10 mL
Salt	¼ tsp.	1 mL
Chopped walnuts	½ cup	125 mL
Chopped maraschino cherries	⅔ cup	150 mL

Combine margarine, sugar and egg in large bowl. Beat together until smooth. Add milk, cherry juice and almond flavoring.

Combine flour, baking powder and salt in medium bowl. Stir in walnuts and cherries. Pour into egg mixture. Stir just to moisten. Spoon into greased 9 x 5 x 3 inch (22 x 2.5 x 7.5 cm) loaf pan. Bake in 350°F (175°C) oven for 45 to 60 minutes until wooden pick inserted in center comes out clean. Cool in pan for 10 minutes. Remove from pan to rack to cool completely. Cuts into 18 slices.

1 slice: 177 Calories; 5.6 g Total Fat; 81 mg Sodium; 3 g Protein; 29 g Carbohydrate; 1 g Dietary Fiber

BARM BRACK

Plan to make this loaf the night before you want to serve it. You will find this a moist loaf.

Cold prepared tea	1 cup	250 mL
Raisins	1 cup	250 mL
Cut mixed peel	½ cup	125 mL
Currants	½ cup	125 mL
Granulated sugar	1 cup	250 mL
Large egg	1	1
Hard margarine (or butter), melted	¼ cup	60 mL
All-purpose flour	2 cups	500 mL
Baking powder	1 tsp.	5 mL
Baking soda	¼ tsp.	1 mL
Salt	¼ tsp.	1 mL

Combine tea, raisins, mixed peel, currants and sugar in large bowl. Cover. Let stand overnight.

Next morning, beat egg in small bowl until frothy. Stir egg and margarine into fruit mixture.

Combine remaining 4 ingredients in small bowl. Add to fruit batter. Stir until well blended. Spoon into greased 9 x 5 x 3 inch (22 x 12.5 x 7.5 cm) loaf pan. Bake in 350°F (175°C) oven for 60 to 70 minutes. Cool in pan for 10 minutes. Remove from pan to rack to cool completely. Cuts into 18 slices.

1 slice: 182 Calories; 3 g Total Fat; 93 mg Sodium; 2 g Protein; 38 g Carbohydrate; 1 g Dietary Fiber

To prevent nuts, raisins or other fruit from sinking to the bottom of your loaf, coat with the dry ingredients before mixing with the wet. You can also try heating raisins or nuts in the oven for just a moment before stirring into the dry ingredients.

ZUCCHINI COCONUT LOAF

Good, spicy and nice looking. This loaf cuts better the next day.

Currants (or raisins)	½ cup	125 mL
Water	1 cup	250 mL
Large egg	1	1
Cooking oil	½ cup	125 mL
Granulated sugar	1 cup	250 mL
Grated zucchini	1 cup	250 mL
Vanilla	½ tsp.	2 mL
All-purpose flour	1½ cups	375 mL
Baking powder	½ tsp.	2 mL
Baking soda	1 tsp.	5 mL
Salt	½ tsp.	2 mL
Ground cinnamon	¾ tsp.	4 mL
Ground nutmeg	½ tsp.	2 mL
Medium coconut	½ cup	125 mL
Chopped walnuts	½ cup	125 mL

Boil currants in water in small saucepan for 2 minutes. Drain and set aside.

Beat egg, cooking oil and sugar together in large bowl. Stir in zucchini and vanilla.

Measure remaining 8 ingredients into medium bowl. Add currants. Stir to combine thoroughly. Pour all at once over batter. Stir just to moisten. Turn into greased 9 x 5 x 3 inch (22 x 12.5 x 7.5 cm) loaf pan. Bake in 350°F (175°C) oven for 1 hour until wooden pick inserted in center comes out clean. Cool in pan for 10 minutes. Remove from pan to rack to cool completely. Cuts into 18 slices.

1 slice: 195 Calories; 10.3 g Total Fat; 158 mg Sodium; 2 g Protein; 25 g Carbohydrate; 1 g Dietary Fiber

CINNAMON BREAD

As tasty and aromatic as can be! Good bread! Rich enough for lunch.

All-purpose flour	2 cups	500 mL
Granulated sugar	1 cup	250 mL
Baking powder	2 tsp.	10 mL
Baking soda	½ tsp.	2 mL
Ground cinnamon	1½ tsp.	7 mL
Salt	1 tsp.	5 mL
Sour milk (1 tbsp., 15 mL, white vinegar plus milk to make)	1 cup	250 mL
Cooking oil	¼ cup	60 mL
Large eggs	2	2
Vanilla	2 tsp.	10 mL
TOPPING		
Granulated sugar	2 tbsp.	30 mL
Ground cinnamon	1 tsp.	5 mL
Hard margarine (or butter), softened	2 tsp.	10 mL

Measure all 10 ingredients in order given into large bowl. Beat for 3 minutes. Pour into greased 9 x 5 x 3 inch (22 x 2.5 x 7.5 cm) loaf pan. Smooth surface.

Topping: Combine all 3 ingredients in small bowl until mixture is crumbly. Sprinkle over batter. Cut in light swirling motion with knife to give marbled effect. Bake in 350°F (175°C) oven for about 50 minutes until wooden pick inserted in center comes out clean. Cool in pan for 10 minutes. Remove from pan to rack to cool completely. Cuts into 18 slices.

1 slice: 153 Calories; 4.5 g Total Fat; 210 mg Sodium; 3 g Protein; 26 g Carbohydrate; 1 g Dietary Fiber

LEMON RAISIN LOAF

A large, moist loaf and really good! A must to try.

Boiling water	³/₄ cup	175 mL
Raisins	1 cup	250 mL
Hard margarine (or butter), softened	¹/₂ cup	125 mL
Brown sugar, packed	1 cup	250 mL
Large eggs	2	2
Grated peel of 1 lemon		
Lemon juice	3 tbsp.	50 mL
All-purpose flour	2¹/₂ cups	625 mL
Baking powder	1 tsp.	5 mL
Baking soda	1 tsp.	5 mL
Salt	¹/₂ tsp.	2 mL
Chopped walnuts (or other)	¹/₂ cup	125 mL

Pour boiling water over raisins in small saucepan. Bring to a boil. Remove from heat. Cool. Do not drain.

Beat margarine, brown sugar and eggs together well in large bowl. Stir in lemon peel, lemon juice and cooled raisin mixture.

Stir flour, baking powder, baking soda, salt and walnuts together in medium bowl. Add all at once to flour mixture, stirring until combined. Pour into greased 9 x 5 x 3 inch (22 x 12.5 x 7.5 cm) loaf pan. Bake in 350°F (175°C) oven for about 1 hour until wooden pick inserted in center comes out clean. Cool in pan for 10 minutes. Remove from pan to rack to cool completely. Cuts into 18 slices.

1 slice: 223 Calories; 8.5 g Total Fat; 229 mg Sodium; 3 g Protein; 35 g Carbohydrate; 1 g Dietary Fiber

ORANGE PUMPKIN LOAF

Serve with an orange cream spread, butter or leave plain. It is a moist loaf.

Hard margarine (or butter), softened	¹/₃ cup	75 mL
Granulated sugar	1¹/₃ cups	325 mL
Large eggs	2	2
Canned pumpkin (without spices)	1 cup	250 mL
Water	¹/₃ cup	75 mL
Medium orange	1	1
All-purpose flour	2 cups	500 mL
Baking soda	1 tsp.	5 mL
Baking powder	¹/₂ tsp.	2 mL
Salt	³/₄ tsp.	4 mL
Ground cinnamon	¹/₂ tsp.	2 mL
Ground cloves	¹/₂ tsp.	2 mL
Chopped nuts	¹/₂ cup	125 mL
Raisins (or chopped dates)	¹/₂ cup	125 mL

Cream margarine and sugar together well in large bowl. Add eggs. Beat together lightly. Stir in pumpkin and water.

Cut orange into quarters and remove seeds. Put entire orange into blender or grinder and process. Stir into batter.

Combine remaining 8 ingredients in medium bowl. Mix well. Stir into batter. Spoon into greased 9 x 5 x 3 inch (22 x 12.5 x 7.5 cm) loaf pan. Bake in 350°F (175°C) oven for 1 hour until wooden pick inserted in center comes out clean. Cool in pan for 10 minutes. Remove from pan to rack to cool completely. Cuts into 18 slices.

1 slice: 199 Calories; 6.7 g Total Fat; 241 mg Sodium; 3 g Protein; 33 g Carbohydrate; 2 g Dietary Fiber

FRUIT BREAD

A very pretty loaf with fruit in a light colored background.

All-purpose flour	2 cups	500 mL
Granulated sugar	¾ cup	175 mL
Baking powder	3½ tsp.	17 mL
Salt	¾ tsp.	4 mL
Diced candied pineapple	¼ cup	60 mL
Raisins (or currants)	½ cup	125 mL
Chopped glazed cherries	½ cup	125 mL
Large eggs	2	2
Milk	1 cup	250 mL
Cooking oil	¼ cup	60 mL

Measure first 7 ingredients into large bowl. Stir together thoroughly. Make a well in center.

Beat eggs in small bowl until frothy. Mix in milk and cooking oil. Pour into well in flour mixture. Stir just to moisten. Pour into greased 9 x 5 x 3 inch (22 x 12.5 x 7.5 cm) loaf pan. Bake in 350°F (175°C) oven for 1 hour. Cool in pan for 10 minutes. Remove from pan to rack to cool completely. Cuts into 18 slices.

1 slice: 171 Calories; 4.1 g Total Fat; 132 mg Sodium; 3 g Protein; 31 g Carbohydrate; 1 g Dietary Fiber

HOVIS-LIKE BREAD

A heavy bread. No added fat is required. Combine dry ingredients early in the day, or make bread ahead and freeze.

Whole wheat (or graham) flour	2 cups	500 mL
All-purpose flour	½ cup	125 mL
Wheat germ	½ cup	125 mL
Brown sugar, packed	2 tbsp.	30 mL
Baking soda	½ tsp.	2 mL
Baking powder	¼ tsp.	1 mL
Salt	½ tsp.	2 mL
Milk	1¾ cups	425 mL

Measure first 7 ingredients into large bowl. Stir together.

Add milk. Mix. Turn into greased 8 x 4 x 3 inch (20 x 10 x 7.5 cm) loaf pan. Bake in 350°F (175°C) oven for about 1½ hours. Cool in pan for 5 minutes. Remove from pan to rack to cool completely. Cuts into 12 slices.

1 slice: 84 Calories; 0.9 g Total Fat; 127 mg Sodium; 4 g Protein; 16 g Carbohydrate; 2 g Dietary Fiber

APPLE LOAF

A tender loaf with a delicate apple flavor.

Hard margarine (or butter), softened	½ cup	125 mL
Granulated sugar	1 cup	250 mL
Large eggs	2	2
Vanilla	1 tsp.	5 mL
Milk	⅓ cup	75 mL
Coarsely grated, unpeeled tart apple, (such as Granny Smith), packed	1 cup	250 mL
All-purpose flour	2 cups	500 mL
Baking powder	1 tsp.	5 mL
Baking soda	½ tsp.	2 mL
Salt	½ tsp.	2 mL
Chopped walnuts	½ cup	125 mL

Combine margarine, sugar and 1 egg in large bowl. Beat until smooth. Add remaining egg and beat together well. Stir in vanilla and milk.

Stir apple into margarine mixture.

Combine flour, baking powder, baking soda, salt and walnuts in small bowl. Add to batter. Stir just to moisten. Scrape into greased 9 x 5 x 3 inch (22 x 12.5 x 7.5 cm) loaf pan. Bake in 350°F (175°C) oven for about 1 hour until wooden pick inserted in center comes out clean. Cool in pan for 10 minutes. Remove from pan to rack to cool completely. Cuts into 18 slices.

1 slice: 186 Calories; 8.5 g Total Fat; 188 mg Sodium; 3 g Protein; 25 g Carbohydrate; 1 g Dietary Fiber

BANNOCK–OFF THE TRAIL

An excellent variation of the original "on the trail" recipe.

All-purpose flour	2¹⁄₂ cups	625 mL
Granulated sugar	3 tbsp.	50 mL
Baking powder	2 tbsp.	30 mL
Salt	1 tsp.	5 mL
Hard margarine (or butter)	2 tbsp.	30 mL
Mashed potato	1 cup	250 mL
Milk	1 cup	250 mL

Combine flour, sugar, baking powder and salt in large bowl. Cut in margarine until mixture is very crumbly.

Add potato. Mix well.

Pour in milk. Stir with fork to form soft ball. Turn out onto lightly floured surface. Knead about 10 times. Place on ungreased baking sheet. Pat down to ³⁄₄ to 1 inch (2 to 2.5 cm) thick. Bake in 400°F (205°C) oven for about 20 minutes until well browned. Cuts into12 pieces.

1 piece: 161 Calories; 2.5 g Total Fat; 270 mg Sodium; 4 g Protein; 30 g Carbohydrate; 1 g Dietary Fiber

Variation: Omit sugar. Add 2 tbsp. (30 mL) molasses.

NUTTY RAISIN BREAD

Try this instead of regular bread. Good toasted too.

Large egg	1	1
Milk	1 cup	250 mL
Cooking oil	1 tbsp.	15 mL
Coarsely chopped raisins	1 cup	250 mL
Chopped walnuts	1 cup	250 mL
All-purpose flour	1¹⁄₂ cups	375 mL
Whole wheat flour	1¹⁄₂ cups	375 mL
Baking powder	1 tbsp.	15 mL
Salt	1 tsp.	5 mL

Beat egg in medium bowl. Add milk, cooking oil, raisins and walnuts.

Add remaining 4 ingredients. Stir just to moisten. Dough will be stiff. Turn into greased 9 x 5 x 3 inch (22 x 12.5 x 7.5 cm) loaf pan. Pat top smooth. Let stand for 20 minutes at room temperature. Bake in 350°F (175°C) oven for about 40 minutes. Cool in pan for 10 minutes. Remove from pan to rack to cool completely. Cuts into 12 slices.

1 slice: 251 Calories; 9.3 g Total Fat; 250 mg Sodium; 7 g Protein; 38 g Carbohydrate; 4 g Dietary Fiber

FRUIT AND NUT LOAF

A fruited, light colored loaf. Very pretty when cut.

Hard margarine (or butter), softened	¹⁄₂ cup	125 mL
Granulated sugar	1 cup	250 mL
Large eggs	2	2
Milk	1 cup	250 mL
Vanilla	1 tsp.	5 mL
Almond flavoring	¹⁄₂ tsp.	2 mL
All-purpose flour	2¹⁄₈ cups	525 mL
Baking powder	2 tsp.	10 mL
Salt	¹⁄₂ tsp.	2 mL
Cut glazed mixed fruit	³⁄₄ cup	175 mL
Raisins (or currants)	³⁄₄ cup	175 mL
Chopped almonds	¹⁄₂ cup	125 mL

Cream margarine and sugar together in large bowl. Beat in eggs, 1 at a time, until smooth. Stir in milk, vanilla and almond flavoring.

Combine flour, baking powder and salt in medium bowl. Stir in fruit, raisins and almonds. Add all at once to egg mixture. Stir just to moisten. Turn into greased 9 x 5 x 3 inch (22 x 12.5 x 7.5 cm) loaf pan. Bake in 350°F (175°C) oven for 1 hour until wooden pick inserted in center comes out clean. Cool in pan for 10 minutes. Remove from pan to rack to cool completely. Cuts into 18 slices.

1 slice: 234 Calories; 8.3 g Total Fat; 162 mg Sodium; 4 g Protein; 37 g Carbohydrate; 1 g Dietary Fiber

CHERRY SPICE LOAF

Looks pretty when sliced. Tastes good.

Large eggs	2	2
Granulated sugar	1 cup	250 mL
Cooking oil	1/2 cup	125 mL
Milk	3/4 cup	175 mL
Almond flavoring	1/2 tsp.	2 mL
All-purpose flour	2 cups	500 mL
Ground cinnamon	1 tsp.	5 mL
Baking powder	1 1/2 tsp.	7 mL
Baking soda	1/2 tsp.	2 mL
Salt	1/4 tsp.	1 mL
Chopped dates	1/2 cup	125 mL
Glazed cherries	1/2 cup	125 mL
Raisins	1/2 cup	125 mL
Chopped walnuts	1/2 cup	125 mL

Beat eggs together lightly in large bowl. Beat in sugar and cooking oil. Slowly add milk and almond flavoring.

Combine flour, cinnamon, baking powder, baking soda and salt in medium bowl. Stir in dates, cherries, raisins and walnuts. Add to egg mixture. Stir just to moisten. Spoon into greased 9 x 5 x 3 inch (22 x 12.5 x 7.5 cm) loaf pan. Bake in 350°F (175°C) oven for 1 hour until wooden pick inserted in center comes out clean. Cool in pan for 10 minutes. Remove from pan to rack to cool completely. Cuts into 18 slices.

1 slice: 235 Calories; 9.5 g Total Fat; 91 mg Sodium; 3 g Protein; 35 g Carbohydrate; 1 g Dietary Fiber

Save hard margarine or butter wrappers and use to grease your baking pans. Store wrappers in a plastic bag in the refrigerator until ready to use.

MERRY FRUIT BREAD

Makes enough pretty slices to fill a plate. Makes a large loaf.

Large eggs	3	3
Granulated sugar	1 cup	250 mL
Cooking oil	1/2 cup	125 mL
Milk	1/2 cup	125 mL
Vanilla	1 tsp.	5 mL
Grated carrot	1 cup	250 mL
All-purpose flour	2 1/2 cups	625 mL
Baking powder	1 tsp.	5 mL
Baking soda	1 tsp.	5 mL
Ground cinnamon	1/2 tsp.	2 mL
Salt	1/2 tsp.	2 mL
Flaked or medium coconut	1 cup	250 mL
Chopped glazed cherries	1/2 cup	125 mL
Raisins	1/2 cup	125 mL
Chopped walnuts (or almonds)	1/2 cup	125 mL

Beat eggs together in large bowl until frothy. Add sugar and cooking oil. Beat to blend. Stir in milk, vanilla and carrot.

Measure remaining 9 ingredients into medium bowl. Mix well to combine evenly. Add all at once to egg mixture. Stir just to moisten. Turn into greased 9 x 5 x 3 inch (22 x 12.5 x 7.5 cm) loaf pan. Bake in 350°F (175°C) oven for 1 hour until wooden pick inserted in center comes out clean. Cool in pan for 10 minutes. Remove from pan to rack to cool completely. Cuts into 18 slices.

1 slice: 277 Calories; 13.2 g Total Fat; 172 mg Sodium; 4 g Protein; 37 g Carbohydrate; 1 g Dietary Fiber

Pictured on page 71.

FAVORITE NUT

It will be your favorite nut too. Superb flavor.

Cream cheese, softened	8 oz.	250 g
Granulated sugar	1/3 cup	75 mL
Large egg	1	1
Large eggs	2	2
Cooking oil	1/2 cup	125 mL
Milk	1/2 cup	125 mL
Grated lemon peel	1 tsp.	5 mL
All-purpose flour	2 1/4 cups	560 mL
Granulated sugar	1/3 cup	75 mL
Brown sugar, packed	1/3 cup	75 mL
Baking soda	1 tsp.	5 mL
Salt	1 tsp.	5 mL
Chopped walnuts	1 cup	250 mL

Combine cream cheese, first amount of sugar and 1 egg in small bowl. Beat together well. Set aside.

Beat remaining eggs together in small bowl until frothy. Mix in cooking oil, milk and lemon peel.

Measure remaining 6 ingredients into medium bowl. Stir to mix well. Add all at once to egg mixture. Stir just to moisten. Spoon 1/2 of batter into greased 9 x 5 x 3 inch (22 x 12.5 x 7.5 cm) loaf pan. Spoon on cream cheese mixture. Cover with remaining 1/2 of batter by dropping small spoonfuls here and there. Bake in 350°F (175°C) oven for 1 hour until wooden pick inserted in center comes out clean. Cool in pan for 15 minutes. Remove from pan to rack to cool completely. Cuts into 18 slices.

1 slice: 274 Calories; 16.9 g Total Fat; 284 mg Sodium; 5 g Protein; 27 g Carbohydrate; 1 g Dietary Fiber

BANANA BREAD

An old standby. Quite dark with lots of flecks.

Hard margarine (or butter), softened	1/2 cup	125 mL
Granulated sugar	1 cup	250 mL
Large eggs	2	2
Mashed ripe banana (about 3 medium)	1 cup	250 mL
All-purpose flour	2 cups	500 mL
Baking soda	1 tsp.	5 mL
Baking powder	1/2 tsp.	2 mL
Salt	1/2 tsp.	2 mL
Chopped walnuts	1 cup	250 mL

Cream margarine and sugar together in medium bowl. Add eggs, 1 at a time, beating until smooth. Blend in banana.

Stir flour, baking soda, baking powder, salt and walnuts together in small bowl. Add to banana mixture. Stir just to moisten. Scrape into greased 9 x 5 x 3 inch (22 x 12.5 x 7.5 cm) loaf pan. Bake in 350°F (175°C) oven for about 1 hour until wooden pick inserted in center comes out clean. Cool in pan for 10 minutes. Remove from pan to rack to cool completely. Cuts into 18 slices.

1 slice: 215 Calories; 10.7 g Total Fat; 224 mg Sodium; 3 g Protein; 27 g Carbohydrate; 1 g Dietary Fiber

BANANA CHIP BREAD: Add 3/4 cup (175 mL) semisweet chocolate chips.

If your bananas ripen before you are ready to use in a recipe, place them, unpeeled, in the freezer. When you are ready to use, thaw and drain excess liquid. Mash and measure as directed.

DATE PINEAPPLE LOAF

A delightful combination, lighter colored than most date loaves.

Canned crushed pineapple, with juice	1 cup	250 mL
Chopped dates	1 cup	250 mL
Baking soda	1 tsp.	5 mL
Hard margarine (or butter), softened	1/4 cup	60 mL
Liquid honey (or 3/4 cup, 175 mL, granulated sugar)	1/2 cup	125 mL
Large egg	1	1
Vanilla	1 tsp.	5 mL
All-purpose flour	2 cups	500 mL
Baking powder	2 tsp.	10 mL
Salt	1/2 tsp.	2 mL

Heat pineapple with juice in medium saucepan until hot. Remove from heat. Add dates and baking soda. Stir. Cool.

Beat margarine, honey, egg and vanilla together in large bowl. Stir in pineapple mixture.

Mix flour, baking powder and salt in small bowl. Add to batter. Stir just to moisten. Spoon into greased 9 × 5 × 3 inch (22 × 12.5 × 7.5 cm) loaf pan. Bake in 350°F (175°C) oven for 1 hour until wooden pick inserted in center comes out clean. Cool in pan for 10 minutes. Remove from pan to rack to cool completely. Cuts into 18 slices.

1 slice: 146 Calories; 3.2 g Total Fat; 190 mg Sodium; 2 g Protein; 28 g Carbohydrate; 1 g Dietary Fiber

CORN BREAD

Serve warm wedges for a definite hit. This freezes well.

All-purpose flour	1 1/4 cups	300 mL
Cornmeal	3/4 cup	175 mL
Granulated sugar	2 tbsp.	30 mL
Baking powder	1 tbsp.	15 mL
Salt	1 tsp.	5 mL
Hard margarine (or butter)	1/4 cup	60 mL
Milk	7/8 cup	200 mL

Measure all 7 ingredients into medium bowl. Beat together until blended. Turn into greased 8 inch (20 cm) round cake pan. Bake in 400°F (205°C) oven for 20 to 25 minutes until wooden pick inserted in center comes out clean. Cuts into 12 wedges.

1 wedge: 138 Calories; 4.6 g Total Fat; 288 mg Sodium; 3 g Protein; 21 g Carbohydrate; 1 g Dietary Fiber

PINEAPPLE BREAD

A moist, tasty loaf. Try a cream cheese spread.

Large eggs	2	2
Hard margarine (or butter), melted	1/2 cup	125 mL
Granulated sugar	1 cup	250 mL
Canned crushed pineapple, with juice	1 cup	250 mL
Vanilla	1 tsp.	5 mL
All-purpose flour	2 1/2 cups	625 mL
Baking powder	1 tbsp.	15 mL
Baking soda	1/2 tsp.	2 mL
Salt	3/4 tsp.	4 mL
Chopped walnuts (or pecans)	1/2 cup	125 mL

Beat eggs together lightly in large bowl. Add margarine and sugar. Beat until smooth. Stir in pineapple with juice and vanilla.

Combine flour, baking powder, baking soda, salt and walnuts in medium bowl. Stir well. Add to pineapple mixture. Stir just to moisten. Pour into greased 9 × 5 × 3 inch (22 × 12.5 × 7.5 cm) loaf pan. Bake in 350°F (175°C) oven for 1 hour until wooden pick inserted in center comes out clean. Cool in pan for 10 minutes. Remove from pan to rack to cool completely. Cuts into 18 slices.

1 slice: 199 Calories; 8 g Total Fat; 220 mg Sodium; 3 g Protein; 29 g Carbohydrate; 1 g Dietary Fiber

PINEAPPLE CHEESE LOAF: Omit nuts. Add 1 cup (250 mL) grated sharp Cheddar cheese.

PINEAPPLE RAISIN/DATE LOAF: Add 1 cup (250 mL) raisins or chopped dates.

RAISIN LOAF

This light colored, small loaf recipe comes from New Zealand. The flavor is best if eaten the day after baking.

Hard margarine (or butter), softened	¼ cup	60 mL
Granulated sugar	¾ cup	175 mL
Large eggs	2	2
Milk	1 cup	250 mL
Vanilla	1 tsp.	5 mL
All-purpose flour	2 cups	500 mL
Baking powder	2 tsp.	10 mL
Salt	½ tsp.	2 mL
Light raisins	½ cup	125 mL
Dark raisins	½ cup	125 mL

Combine margarine, sugar and 1 egg in large bowl. Beat together well. Beat in second egg. Stir in milk and vanilla.

Measure flour, baking powder and salt into medium bowl. Stir in raisins. Pour all at once into batter. Stir just to moisten. Spoon into greased 9 x 5 x 3 inch (22 x 12.5 x 7.5 cm) loaf pan. Bake in 350°F (175°C) oven for 1 hour until wooden pick inserted in center comes out clean. Cool for 10 minutes. Remove from pan to rack to cool completely. Cuts into 16 slices.

1 slice: 172 Calories; 4.1 g Total Fat; 141 mg Sodium; 3 g Protein; 31 g Carbohydrate; 1 g Dietary Fiber

RYE BREAD

A no-yeast loaf that fills the air with a great aroma as it bakes. Good with soup.

Rye flour	2½ cups	625 mL
All-purpose flour	1 cup	250 mL
Baking powder	2 tsp.	10 mL
Baking soda	1 tsp.	5 mL
Large egg	1	1
Cooking (or fancy) molasses	½ cup	125 mL
Sour milk (1 tbsp., 15 mL, white vinegar plus milk to make)	1¼ cups	300 mL

Mix first 4 ingredients in large bowl.

Beat egg in small bowl. Add molasses and sour milk. Mix. Add to dry ingredients. Stir to mix. Scrape into greased 9 x 5 x 3 inch (22 x 12.5 x 7.5 cm) loaf pan. Bake in 350°F (175°C) oven for 45 minutes until wooden pick inserted near center comes out clean. Remove from pan to rack to cool. Cuts into 12 slices.

1 slice: 174 Calories; 1.2 g Total Fat; 138 mg Sodium; 5 g Protein; 37 g Carbohydrate; 4 g Dietary Fiber

COCOA DATE LOAF

A moist loaf and a good keeper.

Chopped pitted dates	1¼ cups	300 mL
Boiling water	1 cup	250 mL
Baking soda	1 tsp.	5 mL
Hard margarine (or butter), softened	2 tbsp.	30 mL
Granulated sugar	¾ cup	175 mL
Large egg	1	1
Vanilla	1 tsp.	5 mL
All-purpose flour	1¾ cups	425 mL
Cocoa	3 tbsp.	50 mL
Salt	¼ tsp.	1 mL
Chopped walnuts (optional)	½ cup	125 mL

Place dates in small bowl. Add boiling water and baking soda. Stir. Set aside.

Cream margarine and sugar together well in large bowl. Beat in egg and vanilla. Add date mixture. Stir.

Add flour, cocoa and salt. Stir just to moisten.

Stir in walnuts. Turn into greased 9 x 5 x 3 inch (22 x 12.5 x 7.5 cm) loaf pan. Bake in center of 350°F (175°C) oven for about 1 hour until wooden pick inserted in center comes out clean. Cool in pan for 15 minutes. Remove from pan to rack to cool completely. Cuts into 18 slices.

1 slice: 122 Calories; 1.7 g Total Fat; 124 mg Sodium; 2 g Protein; 26 g Carbohydrate; 2 g Dietary Fiber

THE GREAT PUMPKIN

The cream cheese contributes to the excellence of this loaf.

Cream cheese, softened	4 oz.	125 g
Hard margarine (or butter), softened	¼ cup	60 mL
Granulated sugar	1¼ cups	300 mL
Large eggs	2	2
Canned pumpkin (without spices)	1 cup	250 mL
All-purpose flour	1¾ cups	425 mL
Baking soda	1 tsp.	5 mL
Baking powder	¼ tsp.	1 mL
Salt	½ tsp.	2 mL
Ground cinnamon	½ tsp.	2 mL
Ground cloves	¼ tsp.	1 mL
Chopped walnuts	½ cup	125 mL

Combine cream cheese, margarine and sugar in medium bowl. Cream together well. Beat in eggs, 1 at a time, until blended. Mix in pumpkin.

Combine remaining 7 ingredients in small bowl. Stir until thoroughly mixed. Add all at once over batter. Stir just to moisten. Spoon into greased 9 x 5 x 3 inch (22 x 12.5 x 7.5 cm) loaf pan. Bake in 350°F (175°C) oven for 60 to 70 minutes until wooden pick inserted in center comes out clean. Cool in pan for 10 minutes. Remove from pan to rack to cool completely. Cuts into 18 slices.

1 slice: 189 Calories; 8.2 g Total Fat; 213 mg Sodium; 3 g Protein; 27 g Carbohydrate; 1 g Dietary Fiber

PUMPKIN LOAF

Good flavor, good color and good size. A winner.

Large eggs	2	2
Granulated sugar	1¼ cups	300 mL
Cooking oil	½ cup	125 mL
Water	⅓ cup	75 mL
Canned pumpkin (without spices)	1 cup	250 mL
All-purpose flour	2 cups	500 mL
Baking soda	1 tsp.	5 mL
Baking powder	½ tsp.	2 mL
Salt	½ tsp.	2 mL
Ground cinnamon	1 tsp.	5 mL
Ground nutmeg	¾ tsp.	4 mL
Ground allspice	½ tsp.	2 mL
Chopped walnuts	½ cup	125 mL
Raisins	½ cup	125 mL

Beat eggs together in large bowl until frothy. Add sugar, cooking oil, water and pumpkin. Beat together well.

Add remaining 9 ingredients. Stir just to moisten. Turn into greased 9 x 5 x 3 inch (22 x 12.5 x 7.5 cm) pan. Bake in 350°F (175°C) oven for 60 to 65 minutes until wooden pick inserted in center comes out clean. Let stand for 10 minutes. Remove from pan to rack to cool completely. Cuts into 18 slices.

1 slice: 217 Calories; 9.5 g Total Fat; 161 mg Sodium; 3 g Protein; 31 g Carbohydrate; 1 g Dietary Fiber

Muffins

uffins can be eaten any time! Enjoy a sweet *Banana Chip Muffin*, page 81, as a mid-morning snack. Savory *Blue Corn Muffins*, page 79, add punch to an on-the-go lunch. Make a variety of muffins and keep in the freezer for an instant breakfast or quick snack. Pack muffins in a picnic lunch, or delight your co-workers with a freshly made batch.

APPLE STREUSEL MUFFINS

This fancy muffin is the "icing on the cake." Good.

TOPPING

Brown sugar, packed	½ cup	125 mL
All-purpose flour	¼ cup	60 mL
Hard margarine (or butter), softened	¼ cup	60 mL
Ground cinnamon	¼ tsp.	1 mL
All-purpose flour	1½ cups	375 mL
Granulated sugar	½ cup	125 mL
Baking powder	1 tbsp.	15 mL
Salt	½ tsp.	2 mL
Large egg	1	1
Milk	⅔ cup	150 mL
Cooking oil	¼ cup	60 mL
Grated cooking apple, (such as McIntosh), with or without peel, packed	¾ cup	175 mL

Topping: Mix brown sugar, flour, margarine and cinnamon in small bowl until mixture is crumbly. Set aside.

Stir flour, sugar, baking powder and salt together in large bowl. Make a well in center.

Beat egg, milk and cooking oil together in small bowl. Stir in apple. Pour into well in flour mixture. Stir just to moisten. Fill greased muffin cups ¾ full. Sprinkle with topping. Bake in 400°F (205°C) oven for 15 to 20 minutes until wooden pick inserted in several muffins comes out clean. Cool in pan for 5 minutes. Remove from pan to rack to cool completely. Makes 12 muffins.

1 muffin: 238 Calories; 9.7 g Total Fat; 181 mg Sodium; 3 g Protein; 35 g Carbohydrate; 1 g Dietary Fiber

Pictured on page 17.

PUMPKIN MUFFINS

Moist and tender. A delicious muffin.

All-purpose flour	1½ cups	375 mL
Baking powder	1 tsp.	5 mL
Baking soda	1 tsp.	5 mL
Salt	½ tsp.	2 mL
Ground cinnamon	½ tsp.	2 mL
Ground nutmeg	½ tsp.	2 mL
Ground ginger	½ tsp.	2 mL
Raisins	½ cup	125 mL
Large egg	1	1
Granulated sugar	¼ cup	60 mL
Cooking oil	⅓ cup	75 mL
Canned pumpkin (without spices)	1 cup	250 mL
Milk	½ cup	125 mL

Combine first 8 ingredients in large bowl. Stir together thoroughly. Make a well in center.

Beat egg in small bowl until frothy. Mix in sugar, cooking oil, pumpkin and milk. Pour into well in flour mixture. Stir just to moisten. Batter will be lumpy. Fill greased muffin cups ¾ full. Bake in 400°F (205°C) oven for 15 to 20 minutes until wooden pick inserted in several muffins comes out clean. Cool in pan for 5 minutes. Remove from pan to rack to cool completely. Makes 12 muffins.

1 muffin: 172 Calories; 7.2 g Total Fat; 242 mg Sodium; 3 g Protein; 25 g Carbohydrate; 1 g Dietary Fiber

ORANGE PUMPKIN MUFFINS: Add 1½ tbsp. (25 mL) grated orange peel to batter.

COFFEE CAKE MUFFINS

These provide a taste of coffee cake in smaller servings.

All-purpose flour	1½ cups	375 mL
Baking powder	2 tsp.	10 mL
Salt	½ tsp.	2 mL
Hard margarine (or butter), softened	¼ cup	60 mL
Granulated sugar	½ cup	125 mL
Large egg	1	1
Milk	¾ cup	175 mL
Vanilla	½ tsp.	2 mL
SPICE MIX		
Brown sugar, packed	½ cup	125 mL
All-purpose flour	2 tbsp.	30 mL
Ground cinnamon	1 tsp.	5 mL

Combine flour, baking powder and salt in large bowl. Stir. Make a well in center.

Combine margarine, sugar and egg in small bowl. Beat together well. Mix in milk and vanilla. Pour into well in flour mixture. Stir just to moisten. Spoon part of batter into greased muffin cups, filling to ⅓ full.

Spice Mix: Combine all 3 ingredients in small bowl. Stir well.

Sprinkle spice mix over top. Spoon remaining batter over top, filling to ⅔ full. Bake in 400°F (205°C) oven for 20 to 25 minutes until wooden pick inserted in several muffins comes out clean. Cool in pan for 5 minutes. Remove from pan to rack to cool completely. Makes 12 muffins.

1 muffin: 186 Calories; 4.9 g Total Fat; 181 mg Sodium; 3 g Protein; 33 g Carbohydrate; 1 g Dietary Fiber

Pictured on page 53 and on back cover.

Use an ice-cream scoop to measure an equal amount of batter in each muffin cup.

BRAN MUFFINS

Can easily be doubled for freezing. Top-notch taste. Gail's favorite.

All-purpose flour	1 cup	250 mL
Baking powder	1 tsp.	5 mL
Baking soda	1 tsp.	5 mL
Salt	½ tsp.	2 mL
Raisins	¾ cup	175 mL
Buttermilk (see Note)	1 cup	250 mL
Natural bran	1 cup	250 mL
Cooking oil	⅓ cup	75 mL
Cooking (or fancy) molasses	3 tbsp.	50 mL
Large egg	1	1
Brown sugar, packed	¼ cup	60 mL
Vanilla	½ tsp.	2 mL

Combine flour, baking powder, baking soda, salt and raisins in large bowl. Stir together. Make a well in center.

Stir buttermilk and bran together in small bowl. Let stand for 5 minutes.

Add remaining 5 ingredients to bran mixture in order given. Beat together with spoon until mixed. Pour into well in flour mixture. Stir just to moisten. Batter will be lumpy. Fill greased muffin cups ¾ full. Bake in 375°F (190°C) oven for 20 to 25 minutes until wooden pick inserted in several muffins comes out clean. Cool in pan for 5 minutes. Remove from pan to rack to cool completely. Makes 12 muffins.

Note: To make sour milk, add 1 tbsp. (15 mL) white vinegar to milk.

1 muffin: 184 Calories; 7.4 g Total Fat; 260 mg Sodium; 4 g Protein; 29 g Carbohydrate; 3 g Dietary Fiber

RHUBARB MUFFINS

Golden brown with chunks of red. Use either fresh or frozen rhubarb. These freeze well.

Cooking oil	⅓ cup	75 mL
Brown sugar, packed	1 cup	250 mL
Large egg	1	1
Vanilla	1¼ tsp.	6 mL
Sour milk (2 tsp., 10 mL, white vinegar plus milk to make)	⅔ cup	150 mL
Rhubarb, cut into ¼ inch (6 mm) cubes (see Note)	1⅓ cups	325 mL
Chopped walnuts	⅓ cup	75 mL
All-purpose flour	1⅔ cups	400 mL
Baking powder	¾ tsp.	4 mL
Baking soda	¾ tsp.	4 mL
Salt	¼ tsp.	1 mL

Beat cooking oil and brown sugar together in medium bowl. Beat in egg. Add vanilla and sour milk. Mix.

Add rhubarb and walnuts. Stir.

Stir remaining 4 ingredients together in small bowl. Add all at once to rhubarb mixture. Stir just to moisten. Fill greased muffin cups almost full. Bake in 400°F (205°C) oven for 20 to 25 minutes until wooden pick inserted in several muffins comes out clean. Cool in pan for 5 minutes. Remove from pan to rack to cool completely. Makes 12 muffins.

1 muffin: 238 Calories; 9.6 g Total Fat; 171 mg Sodium; 3 g Protein; 35 g Carbohydrate; 1 g Dietary Fiber

Note: If using frozen rhubarb, thaw completely and drain.

Pictured on page 53 and on back cover.

BLUEBERRY MUFFINS

An old favorite.

All-purpose flour	1¾ cups	425 mL
Baking powder	1 tbsp.	15 mL
Salt	½ tsp.	2 mL
Hard margarine (or butter), softened	¼ cup	60 mL
Granulated sugar	½ cup	125 mL
Large egg	1	1
Milk	¾ cup	175 mL
Vanilla	1 tsp.	5 mL
Blueberries (fresh or frozen)	1 cup	250 mL
All-purpose flour	1 tbsp.	15 mL

Combine first amount of flour, baking powder and salt in large bowl. Stir thoroughly. Make a well in center.

Cream margarine and sugar together in small bowl. Beat in egg until quite smooth. Stir in milk and vanilla. Pour into well in flour mixture. Stir just to moisten. Batter will be lumpy.

Gently stir blueberries and second amount of flour together in small bowl. Fold into batter. Fill greased muffin cups ¾ full. Bake in 400°F (205°C) oven for 25 minutes until nicely browned. Cool in pan for 5 minutes. Remove from pan to rack to cool completely. Makes 16 muffins.

1 muffin: 124 Calories; 3.7 g Total Fat; 135 mg Sodium; 2 g Protein; 20 g Carbohydrate; 1 g Dietary Fiber

OATMEAL MUFFINS

A good rich flavor.

All-purpose flour	1¼ cups	300 mL
Rolled oats (not instant)	1 cup	250 mL
Brown sugar, packed	¼ cup	60 mL
Baking powder	1 tbsp.	15 mL
Salt	½ tsp.	2 mL
Ground cinnamon	¼ tsp.	1 mL
Raisins	¼ tsp.	1 mL
Large egg	1	1
Cooking (or fancy) molasses	2 tbsp.	30 mL
Cooking oil	¼ cup	60 mL
Milk	1 cup	250 mL
Vanilla	1 tsp.	5 mL

Mix first 7 ingredients in large bowl. Make a well in center.

Beat egg in small bowl until frothy. Mix in molasses, cooking oil, milk and vanilla. Pour into well in flour mixture. Stir just to moisten. Batter will be lumpy. Fill greased muffin cups ¾ full. Bake in 400°F (205°C) oven for 20 to 25 minutes until wooden pick inserted in several muffins comes out clean. Cool in pan for 5 minutes. Remove from pan to rack to cool completely. Makes 16 muffins.

1 muffin: 146 Calories; 4.6 g Total Fat; 103 mg Sodium; 3 g Protein; 24 g Carbohydrate; 1 g Dietary Fiber

GINGER MUFFINS

Dark and different. A lunch box surprise. Better double this recipe.

Hard margarine (or butter), softened	¼ cup	60 mL
Granulated sugar	¼ cup	60 mL
Large egg	1	1
Cooking (or fancy) molasses	½ cup	125 mL
Hot water	¼ cup	60 mL
All-purpose flour	1¾ cups	425 mL
Baking soda	1 tsp.	5 mL
Salt	¼ tsp.	1 mL
Ground cinnamon	½ tsp.	2 mL
Ground ginger	½ tsp.	2 mL
Ground cloves	¼ tsp.	1 mL
Hot water	¼ cup	60 mL

Combine margarine, sugar, egg, molasses and first amount of hot water in large bowl. Beat together well.

Measure next 6 ingredients into same bowl. Stir.

Gradually stir second amount of hot water into batter. Fill greased muffin cups ¾ full. Bake in 400°F (205°C) oven for 20 to 25 minutes until wooden pick inserted in several muffins comes out clean. Cool in pan for 5 minutes. Remove from pan to rack to cool completely. Makes 12 muffins.

1 muffin: 167 Calories; 4.7 g Total Fat; 227 mg Sodium; 3 g Protein; 29 g Carbohydrate; 1 g Dietary Fiber

BLUEBERRY LEMON MUFFINS

Exquisite flavor.

Hard margarine (or butter), softened	¼ cup	60 mL
Granulated sugar	⅓ cup	75 mL
Large egg	1	1
Vanilla	1 tsp.	5 mL
Milk	1 cup	250 mL
All-purpose flour	2 cups	500 mL
Baking powder	2 tsp.	10 mL
Salt	½ tsp.	2 mL
Finely grated peel of 1 lemon		
Fresh blueberries (or frozen, not thawed)	1 cup	250 mL

TOPPING

Juice of 1 lemon		
Granulated sugar	¼ cup	60 mL

Cream margarine and sugar together well in medium bowl. Beat in egg. Add vanilla and milk. Stir.

Add next 4 ingredients. Stir just to moisten.

Quickly fold in blueberries. Fill greased muffin cups ¾ full. Bake in 400°F (205°C) oven for 15 to 20 minutes until wooden pick inserted in several muffins comes out clean. Cool in pan for 5 minutes. Remove from pan to rack to cool completely.

Topping: Stir lemon juice and sugar together in small saucepan on medium until sugar is dissolved. Brush over hot muffins. Makes 12 muffins.

1 muffin: 184 Calories; 5 g Total Fat; 181 mg Sodium; 4 g Protein; 31 g Carbohydrate; 1 g Dietary Fiber

Pictured on page 89.

MUFFINS

A plain muffin that is especially good for meals or snacks.

All-purpose flour	1¾ cups	425 mL
Granulated sugar	2 tbsp.	30 mL
Baking powder	1 tsp.	5 mL
Baking soda	½ tsp.	2 mL
Salt	½ tsp.	2 mL
Large egg	1	1
Buttermilk	1 cup	250 mL
Hard margarine (or butter), melted	2 tbsp.	30 mL

Sift first 5 ingredients into medium bowl. Make a well in center.

Beat egg in small bowl until smooth. Add buttermilk and margarine. Stir together. Pour into well in flour mixture. Stir just to moisten. Spray muffin cups with no-stick cooking spray. Fill cups ¾ full. Bake in 400°F (205°C) oven for 15 to 20 minutes until wooden pick inserted in several muffins comes out clean. Cool in pan for 5 minutes. Remove from pan to rack to cool completely. Makes 12 muffins.

1 muffin: 110 Calories; 3 g Total Fat; 221 mg Sodium; 3 g Protein, 18 g Carbohydrate; 1 g Dietary Fiber

1. Zucchini Muffins, page 83
2. Poppy Seed Muffins, page 85
3. Boston Brown Bread, page 52
4. Chili Biscuits, page 10
5. Choco Banana Loaf, page 34
6. Carrot Loaf, page 47
7. Merry Fruit Bread, page 61
8. Apricot Cheese Loaf, page 37
9. Loaded Biscuits, page 14

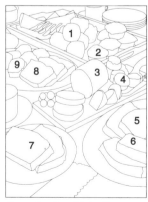

Props Courtesy Of: Le Gnome; The Bay

COTTAGE CHEESE MUFFINS

Moist and simply delicious.

All-purpose flour	1½ cups	375 mL
Baking powder	½ tsp.	2 mL
Baking soda	½ tsp.	2 mL
Salt	½ tsp.	2 mL
Hard margarine (or butter), softened	¼ cup	60 mL
Brown sugar, packed	¾ cup	175 mL
Large egg	1	1
Low-fat cottage cheese	1 cup	250 mL
Skim milk	¼ cup	60 mL
Raisins (or currants)	½ cup	125 mL

Combine first 4 ingredients in medium bowl. Stir. Set aside.

Cream margarine and brown sugar together in large bowl. Beat in egg. Add cottage cheese and milk. Beat to mix thoroughly.

Stir in raisins. Add flour mixture. Stir just to moisten. Spray muffin cups with no-stick cooking spray. Fill greased muffin cups ¾ full. Bake in 375°F (190°C) oven for about 20 minutes until wooden pick inserted in several muffins comes out clean. Cool in pan for 5 minutes. Remove from pan to rack to cool completely. Makes 12 muffins.

1 muffin: 190 Calories; 5 g Total Fat; 312 mg Sodium; 5 g Protein; 33 g Carbohydrate; 1 g Dietary Fiber

BANANA OATMEAL MUFFINS

Tender and scrumptious.

All-purpose flour	1½ cups	375 mL
Rolled oats (not instant)	1 cup	250 mL
Granulated sugar	½ cup	125 mL
Baking powder	2 tsp.	10 mL
Baking soda	1 tsp.	5 mL
Salt	½ tsp.	2 mL
Large eggs	2	2
Cooking oil	¼ cup	60 mL
Milk	¼ cup	60 mL
Mashed ripe banana (about 3 medium)	1 cup	250 mL

Measure first 6 ingredients into large bowl. Stir to mix. Make a well in center.

Beat eggs together in small bowl until frothy. Mix in cooking oil, milk and banana. Pour into well in flour mixture. Stir just to moisten. Batter will be lumpy. Fill greased muffin cups 3/4 full. Bake in 400°F (205°C) oven for 20 to 25 minutes until wooden pick inserted in several muffins comes out clean. Cool in pan for 5 minutes. Remove from pan to rack to cool completely. Makes 12 muffins.

1 muffin: 198 Calories; 6.4 g Total Fat; 244 mg Sodium; 4 g Protein; 31 g Carbohydrate; 2 g Dietary Fiber

CARROT SPICE MUFFINS

Dark and nutritious with spicy overtones.

All-purpose flour	1½ cups	375 mL
Natural bran	1½ cups	375 mL
Wheat germ	¼ cup	60 mL
Brown sugar, packed	½ cup	125 mL
Baking soda	2 tsp.	10 mL
Salt	½ tsp.	2 mL
Ground cinnamon	1 tsp.	5 mL
Ground nutmeg	¼ tsp.	1 mL
Large eggs	2	2
Cooking (or fancy) molasses	¼ cup	60 mL
Cooking oil	¼ cup	60 mL
Milk	1½ cups	375 mL
White vinegar	2 tbsp.	30 mL
Grated carrot	1 cup	250 mL
Chopped walnuts	½ cup	125 mL
Chopped dates (or raisins)	1 cup	250 mL

Combine first 8 ingredients in large bowl. Make a well in center.

Beat eggs together in medium bowl. Add remaining 7 ingredients and stir to mix. Pour into well in flour mixture. Stir just to moisten. Fill greased muffin cups ¾ full. Bake in 400°F (205°C) oven for 20 to 25 minutes until wooden pick inserted in several muffins comes out clean. Cool in pan for 5 minutes. Remove from pan to rack to cool completely. Makes 36 muffins.

1 muffin: 95 Calories; 3.4 g Total Fat; 126 mg Sodium; 2 g Protein; 15 g Carbohydrate; 2 g Dietary Fiber

CHOCOLATE FILLED MUFFINS

These showy muffins would do any tea table proud.

All-purpose flour	2 cups	500 mL
Granulated sugar	3/4 cup	175 mL
Cocoa	1/4 cup	60 mL
Baking powder	1 tbsp.	15 mL
Salt	1/2 tsp.	2 mL
Ground cinnamon	1/2 tsp.	2 mL
Large egg	1	1
Milk	1 cup	250 mL
Cooking oil	1/3 cup	75 mL
FILLING		
Skim milk powder	1/4 cup	60 mL
Hot water	2 tbsp.	30 mL
Hard margarine (or butter)	1 tsp.	5 mL
Almond flavoring	1/4 tsp.	1 mL
Medium coconut	1 cup	250 mL

Combine flour, sugar, cocoa, baking powder, salt and cinnamon in large bowl. Stir. Make a well in center.

Beat egg slightly in small bowl. Stir in milk and cooking oil. Pour into well in flour mixture. Stir just to moisten. Fill greased muffin cups 3/4 full.

Filling: Mix milk powder and hot water in small bowl. Stir vigorously to blend well. Add margarine and almond flavoring. Mix. Stir in coconut. Form into as many balls as muffins. Push down into center of each muffin. Bake in 375°F (190°C) oven for 20 to 25 minutes until wooden pick inserted in several muffins comes out clean. Cool in pan for 5 minutes. Remove from pan to rack to cool completely. Makes16 muffins.

1 muffin: 205 Calories; 9.7 g Total Fat; 116 mg Sodium; 4 g Protein; 27 g Carbohydrate; 2 g Dietary Fiber

Pictured on front cover.

Variation: Omit coconut balls. Use well drained maraschino cherries to push into muffins.

CRANBERRY MUFFINS

The sugared topping finishes these off nicely.

All-purpose flour	2 cups	500 mL
Granulated sugar	1/2 cup	125 mL
Baking powder	4 tsp.	20 mL
Salt	1/2 tsp.	2 mL
Large eggs	2	2
Cooking oil	1/4 cup	60 mL
Milk	1/2 cup	125 mL
Whole cranberry sauce	1 cup	250 mL
TOPPING		
Hard margarine (or butter), melted	2 tsp.	10 mL
Granulated sugar, sprinkle		

Measure flour, sugar, baking powder and salt into large bowl. Stir together thoroughly. Make a well in center.

Beat eggs together in small bowl until frothy. Mix in cooking oil, milk and cranberries. Pour into well in flour mixture. Stir just to moisten. Batter will be lumpy. Fill greased muffins cups 3/4 full. Bake in 400°F (205°C) oven for 20 to 25 minutes until wooden pick inserted in several muffins comes out clean.

Topping: Brush hot muffin tops with margarine. Sprinkle with sugar. Cool in pan for 5 minutes. Remove from pan to rack to cool completely. Makes 18 muffins.

1 muffin: 145 Calories; 4.4 g Total Fat; 99 mg Sodium; 2 g Protein; 24 g Carbohydrate; 1 g Dietary Fiber

FRESH CRANBERRY MUFFINS: Use coarsely chopped or whole cranberries instead of cranberry sauce. Add bit more milk just so batter is not too stiff to spoon out.

BANANA BRAN MUFFINS

Delicious with a hint of chocolate. Dark and devious! The best.

All-purpose flour	1 cup	250 mL
All-bran cereal	1 cup	250 mL
Baking powder	1 tsp.	5 mL
Baking soda	1 tsp.	5 mL
Salt	½ tsp.	2 mL
Cocoa	2 tbsp.	30 mL
Hard margarine (or butter), softened	¼ cup	60 mL
Granulated sugar	½ cup	125 mL
Large eggs	2	2
Sour milk (1 tsp., 5 mL, white vinegar plus milk to make)	¼ cup	60 mL
Mashed ripe banana (about 3 medium)	1 cup	250 mL

Measure first 6 ingredients into large bowl. Stir to combine. Make a well in center.

Cream margarine, sugar and 1 egg together in small bowl until well blended. Beat in second egg. Mix in sour milk and banana. Pour all at once into well in flour mixture. Stir just to moisten. Batter will be lumpy. Fill greased muffin cups ¾ full. Bake in 400°F (205°C) oven for 20 to 25 minutes until wooden pick inserted in several muffins comes out clean. Cool in pan for 5 minutes. Remove from pan to rack to cool completely. Makes 12 muffins.

1 muffin: 160 Calories; 5.4 g Total Fat; 343 mg Sodium; 4 g Protein; 27 g Carbohydrate; 3 g Dietary Fiber

VANILLA MUFFINS

These muffins go with everything.

Hard margarine (or butter), softened	¼ cup	60 mL
Granulated sugar	⅓ cup	75 mL
Large eggs	2	2
Vanilla	1 tsp.	5 mL
Milk	⅔ cup	150 mL
All-purpose flour	2 cups	500 mL
Baking powder	4 tsp.	20 mL
Salt	1 tsp.	5 mL

Cream margarine and sugar together in medium bowl. Beat in eggs. Add vanilla and milk. Mix.

Add flour, baking powder and salt. Stir just to moisten. Fill greased muffin cups ¾ full. Bake in 400°F (205°C) oven for 20 to 25 minutes until wooden pick inserted in several muffins comes out clean. Cool in pan for 5 minutes. Remove from pan to rack to cool completely. Makes 12 muffins.

1 muffin: 161 Calories; 5.3 g Total Fat; 298 mg Sodium; 4 g Protein; 24 g Carbohydrate; 1 g Dietary Fiber

RICE MUFFINS

Gluten-free containing rice as well as rice flour.

Hard margarine (or butter), softened	¼ cup	60 mL
Granulated sugar	2 tbsp.	30 mL
Large eggs	2	2
Milk	⅔ cup	150 mL
Vanilla	1 tsp.	5 mL
Cooked long grain white rice	1½ cups	375 mL
Brown (or white) rice flour	1¼ cups	300 mL
Cornstarch	¾ cup	175 mL
Gluten-free baking powder	1 tbsp.	15 mL
Salt	½ tsp.	2 mL
Raisins (or currants)	½ cup	125 mL

Cream margarine, sugar and 1 egg together well in medium bowl. Beat in second egg. Add milk, vanilla and rice. Beat on low to mix.

Add rice flour, cornstarch, baking powder and salt. Beat on low just to moisten.

Stir in raisins. Fill greased muffin cups ¾ full. Bake in 350°F (175°C) oven for 20 to 25 minutes until wooden pick inserted in several muffins comes out clean. Cool in pan for 5 minutes. Remove from pan to rack to cool completely. Makes 12 muffins.

1 muffin: 214 Calories; 5.5 g Total Fat; 184 mg Sodium; 4 g Protein; 37 g Carbohydrate; 1 g Dietary Fiber

RAISIN MUFFINS

Good rich color. Loaded with raisins.

Raisins	1½ cups	375 mL
Water	1 cup	250 mL
Hard margarine (or butter), softened	½ cup	125 mL
Brown sugar, packed	¾ cup	175 mL
Large egg	1	1
Vanilla	1 tsp.	5 mL
All-purpose flour	2 cups	500 mL
Baking powder	1 tsp.	5 mL
Baking soda	1 tsp.	5 mL
Salt	¼ tsp.	1 mL
Ground cinnamon	½ tsp.	2 mL
Ground nutmeg	½ tsp.	2 mL

Combine raisins and water in small saucepan. Bring to a boil. Simmer, covered, for 10 minutes until plump and tender. Remove from heat. Remove cover to cool. Drain raisins, measuring and reserving ½ cup (125 mL) juice.

Cream margarine, brown sugar and egg together in large bowl. Add vanilla. Stir raisins into batter.

Measure remaining 6 ingredients into medium bowl. Stir to mix. Add to butter mixture alternately with raisin juice, stirring after each addition until barely blended. Fill greased muffin cups ¾ full. Bake in 375°F (190°C) oven for about 20 minutes until wooden pick inserted in several muffins comes out clean. Cool in pan for 5 minutes. Serve warm. Makes 18 muffins.

1 muffin: *189 Calories; 6 g Total Fat; 187 mg Sodium; 2 g Protein; 33 g Carbohydrate; 1 g Dietary Fiber*

Variation: Chopped nuts are a welcome addition.

RAISIN WHEAT MUFFINS

Contain raisins and walnuts. Moist and tasty.

Large eggs	2	2
Cooking oil	2 tbsp.	30 mL
Sour milk (1 tbsp., 15 mL, white vinegar plus milk to make)	1 cup	250 mL
Baking soda	½ tsp.	2 mL
Raisins	½ cup	125 mL
Chopped walnuts	⅓ cup	75 mL
All-purpose flour	1 cup	250 mL
Whole wheat flour	1 cup	250 mL
Brown sugar, packed	¼ cup	60 mL
Baking powder	2 tsp.	10 mL
Salt	½ tsp.	2 mL

Beat eggs together in large bowl. Add cooking oil.

Stir sour milk and baking soda together in small bowl to dissolve baking soda. Add to egg mixture.

Add raisins and walnuts. Stir. ′

Stir remaining 5 ingredients together in medium bowl. Add to egg mixture. Stir just to moisten. Fill greased muffin cups ¾ full. Bake in 400°F (205°C) oven for about 15 minutes until wooden pick inserted in several muffins comes out clean. Cool in pan for 5 minutes. Remove from pan to rack to cool completely. Makes 12 muffins.

1 muffin: *181 Calories; 6.2 g Total Fat; 200 mg Sodium: 5 g Protein; 28 g Carbohydrate; 2 g Dietary Fiber*

CORN MUFFINS

Very quick to prepare.

All-purpose flour	1¼ cups	300 mL
Cornmeal	⅔ cup	150 mL
Brown sugar, packed	½ cup	125 mL
Baking powder	1 tbsp.	15 mL
Ground cinnamon	1 tsp.	5 mL
Salt	½ tsp.	2 mL
Large egg	1	1
Cooking oil	¼ cup	60 mL
Plain yogurt (or milk)	1 cup	250 mL

Stir first 6 ingredients together in medium bowl. Make a well in center.

Beat egg in small bowl. Add cooking oil and yogurt. Beat together. Pour into well in flour mixture. Stir just to moisten. Fill greased muffin cups ¾ full. Bake in 400°F (205°C) oven for 15 to 20 minutes until wooden pick inserted in several muffins comes out clean. Cool in pan for 5 minutes. Remove from pan to rack to cool completely. Makes 12 muffins.

1 muffin: 181 Calories; 5.9 g Total Fat; 141 mg Sodium; 4 g Protein; 28 g Carbohydrate; 1 g Dietary Fiber

BANANA MUFFINS

Mellow banana flavor.

All-purpose flour	1¾ cups	425 mL
Baking soda	1 tsp.	5 mL
Salt	¼ tsp.	1 mL
Hard margarine (or butter), softened	½ cup	125 mL
Granulated sugar	1¼ cups	300 mL
Large eggs	2	2
Sour cream	¼ cup	60 mL
Mashed ripe banana (about 3 medium)	1 cup	250 mL

Measure flour, baking soda and salt into large bowl. Stir together. Make a well in center.

Cream margarine, sugar and 1 egg together in medium bowl. Beat in second egg. Mix in sour cream and banana. Pour into well in flour mixture. Stir to mix. Batter will be lumpy. Fill greased muffin cups ¾ full. Bake in 400°F (205°C) oven for 20 to 25 minutes until wooden pick inserted in several muffins comes out clean. Cool in pan for 5 minutes. Remove from pan to rack to cool completely. Makes 16 muffins.

1 muffin: 199 Calories; 7.5 g Total Fat; 210 mg Sodium; 3 g Protein; 31 g Carbohydrate; 1 g Dietary Fiber

BRAN MUFFINS

Good texture and flavor.

Natural bran	1 cup	250 mL
Buttermilk	¾ cup	175 mL
Large egg	1	1
Brown sugar, packed	½ cup	125 mL
Hard margarine (or butter), softened	2 tbsp.	30 mL
All-purpose flour	1 cup	250 mL
Baking powder	1 tsp.	5 mL
Baking soda	½ tsp.	2 mL
Salt	½ tsp.	2 mL

Stir bran and buttermilk together in small bowl.

Combine egg, brown sugar and margarine in medium bowl. Beat together until fluffy. Add bran mixture. Stir.

Stir remaining 4 ingredients together in third bowl. Add to batter. Stir just to moisten. Batter will be lumpy. Fill greased muffin cups ¾ full. Bake in 400°F (205°C) oven for 15 to 20 minutes until wooden pick inserted in several muffins comes out clean. Cool in pan for 5 minutes. Remove from pan to rack to cool completely. Makes 12 muffins.

1 muffin: 118 Calories; 2.8 g Total Fat; 217 mg Sodium; 3 g Protein; 22 g Carbohydrate; 3 g Dietary Fiber

NUTTY OAT MUFFINS

Good nutty flavor. Nuts may be increased if desired.

Rolled oats (not instant)	⅓ cup	75 mL
Milk	¾ cup	175 mL
Hard margarine (or butter), softened	½ cup	125 mL
Brown sugar, packed	⅓ cup	75 mL
Large eggs	2	2
Vanilla	½ tsp.	2 mL
All-purpose flour	1½ cups	375 mL
Baking powder	1 tbsp.	15 mL
Salt	¼ tsp.	1 mL
Chopped walnuts	½ cup	125 mL

Combine rolled oats and milk in small bowl. Let stand for 10 minutes.

Cream margarine and brown sugar together in large bowl. Beat in eggs, 1 at a time. Add vanilla and oat mixture. Stir.

Add flour, baking powder, salt and walnuts. Stir just to moisten. Fill greased muffin cups at least ¾ full. Bake in 400°F (205°C) oven for 15 to 20 minutes until wooden pick inserted in several muffins comes out clean. Cool in pan for about 5 minutes. Remove from pan to rack to cool completely. Makes 12 muffins.

1 muffin: 223 Calories; 12.9 g Total Fat; 178 mg Sodium; 5 g Protein; 23 g Carbohydrate; 1 g Dietary Fiber

CRANBERRY MUFFINS

Enjoy these with milk or coffee. Gluten-free.

Hard margarine (or butter), softened	¼ cup	60 mL
Granulated sugar	⅓ cup	75 mL
Large eggs	2	2
Milk	1 cup	250 mL
Vanilla	1 tsp.	5 mL
Rice flour	2 cups	500 mL
Tapioca flour	¼ cup	60 mL
Gluten-free baking powder	1 tbsp.	15 mL
Baking soda	½ tsp.	2 mL
Salt	½ tsp.	2 mL
Halved cranberries (fresh or frozen)	1 cup	250 mL

Cream margarine and sugar together in medium bowl. Beat in eggs, 1 at a time. Add milk and vanilla. Stir. Mixture may curdle.

Add next 5 ingredients. Beat together.

Fold in cranberries. Fill greased muffin cups ¾ full. Bake in 350°F (175°C) oven for about 25 minutes until wooden pick inserted in several muffins comes out clean. Cool in pan for 5 minutes. Remove from pan to rack to cool completely. Makes 12 muffins.

1 muffin: 201 Calories; 5.6 g Total Fat; 244 mg Sodium; 3 g Protein; 34 g Carbohydrate; 1 g Dietary Fiber

If muffins become a little dry in storage, brush with milk and place in a warm oven for 5 to 8 minutes until warmed through.

CHOCOLATE BRAN MUFFINS

Yummy. Drizzle or ice with chocolate and serve with coffee or tea for a special treat.

Hard margarine (or butter), softened	⅓ cup	75 mL
Granulated sugar	¾ cup	175 mL
Large egg	1	1
Milk	1 cup	250 mL
All-bran cereal	1 cup	250 mL
All-purpose flour	1½ cups	375 mL
Cocoa	¼ cup	60 mL
Baking powder	1 tbsp.	15 mL
Salt	½ tsp.	2 mL

Cream margarine and sugar together in large bowl. Beat in egg.

Stir milk and cereal together in small bowl. Let stand for 10 minutes. Add to egg mixture.

Add remaining 4 ingredients. Stir just to moisten. Fill greased muffin cups ¾ full. Bake in 400°F (205°C) oven for about 15 minutes until wooden pick inserted in several muffins comes out clean. Cool in pan for 5 minutes. Remove from pan to rack to cool completely. Makes 12 muffins.

1 muffin: 194 Calories; 6.5 g Total Fat; 250 mg Sodium; 4 g Protein; 33 g Carbohydrate; 3 g Dietary Fiber

WHOLE WHEAT MUFFINS

Can you believe that a muffin so nutritious can taste so delicious?

Whole wheat flour	2 cups	500 mL
Granulated sugar	¼ cup	60 mL
Baking powder	1 tbsp.	15 mL
Salt	½ tsp.	2 mL
Large egg, fork-beaten	1	1
Milk	1 cup	250 mL
Cooking oil	¼ cup	60 mL

Stir flour, sugar, baking powder and salt together in medium bowl. Make a well in center.

Pour egg, milk and cooking oil into well in flour mixture. Stir just to moisten. Fill greased muffin cups ¾ full. Bake in 400°F (205°C) oven for 20 to 25 minutes until wooden pick inserted in several muffins comes out clean. Cool in pan for 5 minutes. Serve warm. Makes 12 muffins.

1 muffin: 148 Calories; 5.9 g Total Fat; 134 mg Sodium; 4 g Protein; 21 g Carbohydrate; 3 g Dietary Fiber

CRANBERRY ORANGE MUFFINS

Good enough to be dessert.

All-purpose flour	2 cups	500 mL
Granulated sugar	½ cup	125 mL
Baking powder	1 tbsp.	15 mL
Salt	½ tsp.	2 mL
Large eggs	2	2
Hard margarine (or butter), melted	¼ cup	60 mL
Grated peel of 1 orange		
Juice of 1 orange plus water to make	1 cup	250 mL
Vanilla	1 tsp.	5 mL
Chopped cranberries, (fresh or frozen, thawed)	1 cup	250 mL

Combine first 4 ingredients in large bowl. Stir. Make a well in center.

Beat eggs together in small bowl. Stir in margarine, orange peel, orange juice and vanilla. Pour into well in flour mixture. Stir just to moisten.

Blot cranberries with paper towel. Fold into batter. Fill greased muffin cups at least ¾ full. Bake in 400°F (205°C) oven for 15 to 20 minutes until wooden pick inserted in several muffins comes out clean. Cool in pan for 5 minutes. Remove from pan to rack to cool completely. Makes 12 muffins.

1 muffin: 172 Calories; 4.8 g Total Fat; 172 mg Sodium; 3 g Protein; 29 g Carbohydrate; 1 g Dietary Fiber

Pictured on front cover.

RASPBERRY CREAM MUFFINS

Strong raspberry flavor and red Christmas color. Serve at brunch, afternoon tea or as a late evening snack.

All-purpose flour	2 cups	500 mL
Baking powder	1 tsp.	5 mL
Baking soda	1/2 tsp.	2 mL
Salt	1/2 tsp.	2 mL
Ground cinnamon	1/4 tsp.	1 mL
Hard margarine (or butter), softened	1 1/2 cups	125 mL
Granulated sugar	2/3 cup	150 mL
Large eggs	2	2
Sour cream	1/2 cup	125 mL
Vanilla	1 tsp.	5 mL
Coarsely chopped frozen raspberries	1 cup	250 mL

Measure first 5 ingredients into small bowl. Stir together well.

Beat margarine and sugar together in medium bowl. Beat in eggs, 1 at a time. Add sour cream and vanilla. Beat to mix. Add flour mixture. Stir just to moisten.

Fold in raspberries. Fill greased muffin cups almost full. Bake in 350°F (175°C) oven for 30 to 35 minutes until golden. Wooden pick inserted in several muffins should come out clean. Cool in pan for 10 minutes. Remove from pan to rack to cool completely. Makes 12 muffins.

1 muffin: 233 Calories; 10.7 g Total Fat; 282 mg Sodium; 4 g Protein; 31 g Carbohydrate; 1 g Dietary Fiber

Pictured on page 35.

BLUE CORN MUFFINS

No, not blue corn—blueberries and cornmeal! An interesting combination.

All-purpose flour	1 1/4 cups	300 mL
Cornmeal	2/3 cup	150 mL
Granulated sugar	1/3 cup	75 mL
Baking powder	1 tbsp.	15 mL
Salt	1/2 tsp.	2 mL
Blueberries (fresh or frozen)	1 cup	250 mL
Large egg	1	1
Cooking oil	1/4 cup	60 mL
Milk	1 cup	250 mL
TOPPING		
Lemon juice	3 tbsp.	50 mL
Granulated sugar	1/4 cup	60 mL

Combine first 6 ingredients in large bowl. Stir together lightly. Make a well in center.

Beat egg in small bowl. Add cooking oil and milk. Stir together. Pour into well in flour mixture. Stir just to moisten. Fill greased muffin cups 3/4 full. Bake in 400°F (205°C) oven for 15 to 20 minutes. Wooden pick inserted in several muffins should come out clean.

Topping: Measure lemon juice and sugar into small saucepan. Heat and stir until sugar is dissolved. Brush over hot muffins, dividing mixture among them. Cool in pan for 5 minutes. Remove from pan to rack to cool completely. Makes 12 muffins.

1 muffin: 187 Calories; 5.8 g Total Fat; 135 mg Sodium; 3 g Protein; 31 g Carbohydrate; 1 g Dietary Fiber

Most muffin recipes can be made in either the regular-size muffin tins or the mini or jumbo. Just remember to add time to the jumbo and cut back on baking time for the mini; the quantity will also change accordingly.

OATMEAL MUFFINS

Try your oatmeal in a muffin instead of a bowl. These are excellent with or without the addition of coconut or dates.

Rolled oats (not instant)	1 cup	250 mL
Buttermilk	1 cup	250 mL
All-purpose flour	1 cup	250 mL
Brown sugar, packed	³/₄ cup	175 mL
Baking powder	1 tsp.	5 mL
Baking soda	¹/₂ tsp.	2 mL
Salt	¹/₄ tsp.	1 mL
Large egg	1	1
Hard margarine (or butter), melted	¹/₄ cup	60 mL
Coconut (or chopped dates), optional	¹/₄ cup	60 mL

Put rolled oats and buttermilk into small bowl. Stir together just to moisten. Let stand.

Measure flour, brown sugar, baking powder, baking soda and salt into large bowl. Stir together to mix. Make a well in center.

Add egg and margarine to oat mixture. Mix well. Pour all at once into well in flour mixture. Stir just to moisten. Fill greased muffin cups ³/₄ full. Bake in 400°F (205°C) oven for about 20 minutes until wooden pick inserted in several muffins comes out clean. Cool in pan for 5 minutes. Remove from pan to rack to cool completely. Makes 12 muffins.

1 muffin: 171 Calories; 4.9 g Total Fat; 192 mg Sodium; 4 g Protein; 28 g Carbohydrate; 1 g Dietary Fiber

PEANUT BUTTER MUFFINS

Nutrition packed in a small package. Serve warm.

All-purpose flour	1¹/₂ cups	375 mL
Granulated sugar	¹/₄ cup	60 mL
Baking powder	1 tbsp.	15 mL
Salt	¹/₂ tsp.	2 mL
All-bran cereal	1 cup	250 mL
Milk	1 cup	250 mL
Large egg	1	1
Smooth peanut butter	¹/₂ cup	125 mL
Cooking oil	¹/₄ cup	60 mL
Milk	¹/₂ cup	125 mL

Combine flour, sugar, baking powder and salt in large bowl. Stir to mix. Make a well in center.

Combine cereal and first amount of milk in medium bowl.

Add egg and peanut butter to cereal mixture. Beat together with spoon to mix. Add cooking oil and second amount of milk. Stir. Pour into well in flour mixture. Stir just to moisten. Batter will be lumpy. Fill greased muffin cups ³/₄ full. Bake in 400°F (205°C) oven for 15 to 20 minutes until wooden pick inserted in several muffins comes out clean. Cool in pan for 5 minutes. Remove from pan to rack to cool completely. Makes 12 muffins.

1 muffin: 222 Calories; 11.5 g Total Fat; 246 mg Sodium; 7 g Protein; 26 g Carbohydrate; 3 g Dietary Fiber

If you have empty muffin cups when baking muffins, fill the empty cups with about ¹/₄ inch (6 mm) water. This will help ensure even baking.

BANANA CHIP MUFFINS

Cake-like texture with the popular banana chocolate taste.

All-purpose flour	1¾ cups	425 mL
Granulated sugar	½ cup	125 mL
Baking powder	1 tbsp.	15 mL
Salt	½ tsp.	2 mL
Semisweet chocolate chips	½ cup	125 mL
Large egg	1	1
Cooking oil	¼ cup	60 mL
Milk	¼ cup	60 mL
Mashed ripe banana (about 3 medium)	1 cup	250 mL

Measure first 5 ingredients into large bowl. Mix thoroughly and make a well in center.

Beat egg in small bowl until frothy. Mix in cooking oil, milk and banana. Pour into well in flour mixture. Stir just to moisten. Batter will be lumpy. Fill greased muffin cups ¾ full. Bake in 400°F (205°C) oven for 20 to 25 minutes until wooden pick inserted in several muffins comes out clean. Cool in pan for 5 minutes. Remove from pan to rack to cool completely. Makes 12 muffins.

1 muffin: 206 Calories; 7.8 g Total Fat; 127 mg Sodium; 3 g Protein; 32 g Carbohydrate; 1 g Dietary Fiber

CHEESE AND BACON MUFFINS

Grab a cup of coffee and one of these muffins— breakfast on the run!

All-purpose flour	2 cups	500 mL
Granulated sugar	2 tbsp.	30 mL
Baking powder	1 tbsp.	15 mL
Salt	¼ tsp.	1 mL
Grated sharp Cheddar cheese	½ cup	125 mL
Bacon slices, cooked and crumbled	4-5	4-5
Large egg, fork-beaten	1	1
Milk	1 cup	250 mL
Cooking oil	¼ cup	60 mL

Measure first 6 ingredients into large bowl. Stir together thoroughly. Make a well in center.

Beat egg with fork in small bowl. Mix in milk and cooking oil. Pour into well in flour mixture. Stir just to moisten. Batter will be lumpy. Fill greased muffin cups ¾ full. Bake in 400°F (205°C) oven for 20 to 25 minutes until wooden pick inserted in several muffins comes out clean. Cool in pan for 5 minutes. Serve warm. Makes 12 muffins.

1 muffin: 180 Calories; 8.4 g Total Fat; 142 mg Sodium; 5 g Protein; 20 g Carbohydrate; 1 g Dietary Fiber

Pictured on page 89.

Variation: Substitute milk with 1 can (10 oz., 284 mL) condensed cream of chicken soup or mushroom soup.

RICE MUFFINS

Flavorful and light.

Egg whites (large), room temperature	2	2
Cooked long grain white rice	1 cup	250 mL
Egg yolk (large)	1	1
Cooking oil	2 tbsp.	30 mL
Skim milk	1 cup	250 mL
Salt	¼ tsp.	1 mL
All-purpose flour	1 cup	250 mL

Beat egg whites together in small bowl until stiff.

Using same beaters, beat rice, egg yolk, cooking oil, skim milk and salt together in medium bowl.

Add flour. Stir. Fold in egg whites. Spray muffin cups with no-stick cooking spray. Fill greased muffins cups ¾ full. Bake in 400°F (205°C) oven for 15 to 20 minutes until wooden pick inserted in several muffins comes out clean. Cool in pan for 5 minutes. Serve warm. Makes 12 muffins.

1 muffin: 99 Calories; 3 g Total Fat; 77 mg Sodium; 2 g Protein; 11 g Carbohydrate; trace Dietary Fiber

CHEESY APPLE MUFFINS

A nice looking muffin.

Hard margarine (or butter), softened	¼ cup	60 mL
Granulated sugar	½ cup	125 mL
Large eggs	2	2
Milk	½ cup	125 mL
Peeled and grated cooking apple (such as McIntosh), packed	1 cup	250 mL
All-purpose flour	1½ cups	375 mL
Quick-cooking rolled oats (not instant)	¾ cup	175 mL
Grated sharp Cheddar cheese	¾ cup	175 mL
Baking powder	1½ tsp.	7 mL
Baking soda	1 tsp.	5 mL
Salt	½ tsp.	2 mL

Cream margarine and sugar together well in medium bowl. Beat in eggs, 1 at a time. Add milk and apple. Stir.

Measure remaining 6 ingredients into small bowl. Stir to distribute evenly. Add to apple mixture. Stir just to moisten. Fill greased muffin cups ¾ full. Bake in 400°F (205°C) oven for 15 to 20 minutes until wooden pick inserted in several muffins comes out clean. Cool in pan for 5 minutes. Remove from pan to rack to cool completely. Makes 12 muffins.

1 muffin: 204 Calories; 8 g Total Fat; 339 mg Sodium; 6 g Protein; 27 g Carbohydrate; 1 g Dietary Fiber

Pictured on page 35.

Variation: After baking for 10 to 12 minutes, sprinkle tops with more grated cheese. Bake for 5 minutes.

BATTER-READY GINGER MUFFINS

Quick to make. Batter can be prepared three weeks ahead of time and kept in the refrigerator. These freeze well too.

Hard margarine (or butter), softened	1½ cups	375 mL
Granulated sugar	1 cup	250 mL
Large eggs	4	4
Cooking (or fancy) molasses	1½ cups	375 mL
Buttermilk	1 cup	250 mL
Vanilla	1½ tsp.	7 mL
All-purpose flour	5¼ cups	1.3 L
Ground cinnamon	1½ tsp.	7 mL
Ground ginger	1½ tsp.	7 mL
Ground nutmeg	½ tsp.	2 mL
Ground cloves	¼ tsp.	1 mL
Salt	¾ tsp.	4 mL
Baking soda	1 tbsp.	15 mL
Raisins	1½ cups	375 mL

Cream margarine and sugar together well in large bowl. Beat in eggs, 1 at a time. Add molasses. Beat to mix. Add buttermilk and vanilla. Mix.

Stir remaining 8 ingredients together well in large bowl. Add to molasses mixture. Stir just to moisten. Store in covered container in refrigerator for up to 3 weeks. Fill greased muffin cups ¾ full. Bake in 400°F (205°C) oven for 15 to 20 minutes until wooden pick inserted in several muffins comes out clean. Cool in pan for 5 minutes. Remove from pan to rack to cool completely. Makes 36 muffins.

1 muffin: 233 Calories; 9 g Total Fat; 269 mg Sodium; 3 g Protein; 36 g Carbohydrate; 1 g Dietary Fiber

FRUITY OATMEAL MUFFINS

So colorful with cranberries peeking through the top.

All-purpose flour	1¼ cups	300 mL
Rolled oats (not instant)	1 cup	250 mL
Brown sugar, packed	¼ cup	60 mL
Baking powder	1 tbsp.	15 mL
Salt	½ tsp.	2 mL
Ground cinnamon	¼ tsp.	1 mL
Large egg	1	1
Liquid honey	2 tbsp.	30 mL
Cooking oil	¼ cup	60 mL
Milk	½ cup	125 mL
Vanilla	1 tsp.	5 mL
Cranberries (fresh or frozen), halved	1 cup	250 mL
Cooking apples (such as McIntosh), peeled, cored and diced	2	2

Combine first 6 ingredients in large bowl. Stir. Make a well in center.

Beat egg in medium bowl until frothy. Mix in honey, cooking oil, milk and vanilla.

Add cranberries and apple to egg mixture. Stir. Pour into well in flour mixture. Stir just to moisten. Fill greased muffin cups ¾ full. Bake in 400°F (205°C) oven for 15 to 20 minutes until wooden pick inserted in several muffins comes out clean. Cool in pan for 5 minutes. Remove from pan to rack to cool completely. Makes 12 muffins.

1 muffin: 180 Calories; 6 g Total Fat; 130 mg Sodium; 4 g Protein; 28 g Carbohydrate; 2 g Dietary Fiber

ZUCCHINI MUFFINS

Ever popular. Good and spicy with whole wheat flour as an extra benefit.

All-purpose flour	1 cup	250 mL
Whole wheat flour	1 cup	250 mL
Baking powder	1½ tsp.	7 mL
Baking soda	½ tsp.	2 mL
Ground cinnamon	1 tsp.	5 mL
Ground allspice	½ tsp.	2 mL
Salt	1 tsp.	5 mL
Large egg	1	1
Cooking oil	¼ cup	60 mL
Granulated sugar	½ cup	125 mL
Grated zucchini, with peel	1 cup	250 mL
Milk	½ cup	125 mL

Measure first 7 ingredients into large bowl. Stir together thoroughly. Make a well in center.

Beat egg in medium bowl until frothy. Mix in cooking oil, sugar, zucchini and milk. Pour into well in flour mixture. Stir just to moisten. Batter will be lumpy. Fill greased muffin cups ¾ full. Bake in 400°F (205°C) oven for 20 to 25 minutes until wooden pick inserted in several muffins comes out clean. Cool in pan for 5 minutes. Serve warm. Makes 12 muffins.

1 muffin: 167 Calories; 5.7 g Total Fat; 297 mg Sodium; 4 g Protein; 26 g Carbohydrate; 2 g Dietary Fiber

Pictured on page 71.

When measuring molasses or honey, coat the inside of the measuring cup with a bit of oil and then rinse with warm water. The sticky ingredients will pour out more easily.

CHRISTMAS FRUIT MUFFINS

Fill a basket with these for Christmas morning breakfast. Very colorful.

All-purpose flour	1¾ cups	425 mL
Baking powder	1 tsp.	5 mL
Baking soda	1 tsp.	5 mL
Salt	½ tsp.	2 mL
Red candied pineapple ring, diced	1	1
Green candied pineapple ring, diced	1	1
Yellow candied pineapple ring, diced	1	1
Chopped pecans	½ cup	125 mL
Hard margarine (or butter), softened	½ cup	125 mL
Granulated sugar	1 cup	250 mL
Large eggs	2	2
Vanilla	1 tsp.	5 mL
Milk	⅔ cup	150 mL

Measure first 8 ingredients into large bowl. Stir. Make a well in center.

Cream margarine and sugar together in small bowl. Beat in eggs, 1 at a time. Add vanilla and milk. Stir. Pour into well in flour mixture. Stir just to moisten. Fill greased muffin cups ¾ full. Bake in 400°F (205°C) oven for 15 to 20 minutes until wooden pick inserted in several muffins comes out clean. Cool in pan for 5 minutes. Remove from pan to rack to cool completely. Makes 12 muffins.

1 muffin: 301 Calories; 12.9 g Total Fat; 343 mg Sodium; 4 g Protein; 43 g Carbohydrate; 1 g Dietary Fiber

G' MORNING MUFFINS

Perfect in the morning with a cup of coffee. Have the dry ingredients combined the night before. These freeze well.

Large egg, fork-beaten	1	1
Canned crushed pineapple, drained, 6 tbsp. (100 mL) juice reserved	14 oz.	398 mL
Grated carrot	½ cup	125 mL
Cooking oil	¼ cup	60 mL
Reserved pineapple juice		
All-purpose flour	1½ cups	375 mL
Quick-cooking rolled oats (not instant)	¾ cup	175 mL
Brown sugar, packed	½ cup	125 mL
Baking powder	1 tbsp.	15 mL
Baking soda	1 tsp.	5 mL
Ground cinnamon	1 tsp.	5 mL
Salt	¼ tsp.	1 mL
Raisins	⅓ cup	75 mL

Stir first 5 ingredients together in medium bowl.

Combine remaining 8 ingredients in large bowl. Stir to mix. Make a well in center. Pour carrot mixture into well. Stir just to moisten. Fill greased muffin cups ¾ full. Bake in 400°F (205°C) oven for 18 to 20 minutes until golden brown. Wooden pick inserted in several muffins should come out clean. Cool in pan for 5 minutes. Remove from pan to rack to cool completely. Makes 12 muffins.

1 muffin: 175 Calories; 5 g Total Fat; 160 mg Sodium; 3 g Protein; 30 g Carbohydrate; 2 g Dietary Fiber

KIWIFRUIT MUFFINS

A different, moist muffin.

All-purpose flour	2 cups	500 mL
Granulated sugar	½ cup	125 mL
Baking powder	1 tbsp.	15 mL
Baking soda	½ tsp.	2 mL
Salt	½ tsp.	2 mL
Kiwifruit, peeled and finely chopped	3	3
Large egg, fork-beaten	1	1
Hard margarine (or butter), melted	¼ cup	60 mL
Milk	⅓ cup	75 mL
Vanilla	1 tsp.	5 mL

Stir first 5 ingredients together in large bowl.

Add kiwifruit. Stir gently. Make a well in center.

Add remaining 4 ingredients to well. Stir just to moisten. Fill greased muffin cups ¾ full. Bake in 400°F (205°C) oven for 15 to 20 minutes until wooden pick inserted in several muffins comes out clean. Cool in pan for 5 minutes. Remove from pan to rack to cool completely. Makes 12 muffins.

1 muffin: 174 Calories; 4.9 g Total Fat; 226 mg Sodium; 3 g Protein; 29 g Carbohydrate; 1 g Dietary Fiber

CORN MUFFINS

Not only different, but excellent as well. Contains sour cream.

All-purpose flour	1 cup	250 mL
Yellow cornmeal	1 cup	250 mL
Granulated sugar	¼ cup	60 mL
Baking powder	1 tsp.	5 mL
Baking soda	1 tsp.	5 mL
Salt	1 tsp.	5 mL
Large eggs	2	2
Sour cream	1 cup	250 mL
Hard margarine (or butter), melted	¼ cup	60 mL

Measure first 6 ingredients into medium bowl. Stir together. Make a well in center.

Beat eggs and sour cream together in small bowl. Add margarine. Mix. Pour into well in flour mixture. Stir just to moisten. Fill greased muffin cups ¾ full. Bake in 425°F (220°C) oven for 15 to 20 minutes until wooden pick inserted in several muffins comes out clean. Cool in pan for 5 minutes. Remove from pan to rack to cool completely. Makes 12 muffins.

1 muffin: 179 Calories; 7.7 g Total Fat; 405 mg Sodium; 4 g Protein; 23 g Carbohydrate; 1 g Dietary Fiber

POPPY SEED MUFFINS

For the best treat going, serve warm with maple butter.

Milk	1¼ cups	300 mL
Poppy seed	¼ cup	60 mL
Hard margarine (or butter), softened	¼ cup	60 mL
Granulated sugar	½ cup	125 mL
Large egg	1	1
Vanilla	1 tsp.	5 mL
All-purpose flour	2 cups	500 mL
Baking powder	1 tbsp.	15 mL
Salt	½ tsp.	2 mL

Combine milk and poppy seed in small bowl. Let stand for about 10 minutes.

Cream margarine, sugar and egg together in second small bowl. Add vanilla. Stir in poppy seed mixture.

Measure flour, baking powder and salt into large bowl. Stir to mix thoroughly. Make a well in center. Pour poppy seed mixture into well. Stir just to moisten. Fill greased muffin cups ¾ full. Bake in 400°F (205°C) oven for 15 to 20 minutes until wooden pick inserted in several muffins comes out clean. Cool in pan for 5 minutes. Serve warm. Makes 12 muffins.

1 muffin: 187 Calories; 6.4 g Total Fat; 185 mg Sodium; 4 g Protein; 28 g Carbohydrate; 1 g Dietary Fiber

Pictured on page 71.

ORANGE BRAN MUFFINS

The orange adds a real tang. A super muffin.

All-purpose flour	1 cup	250 mL
All-bran cereal (or natural bran)	1 cup	250 mL
Baking powder	1 tsp.	5 mL
Baking soda	1 tsp.	5 mL
Salt	¼ tsp.	1 mL
Brown sugar, packed	½ cup	125 mL
Ground nutmeg	⅛ tsp.	0.5 mL
Large egg	1	1
Cooking oil	¼ cup	60 mL
Sour milk (2 tsp., 10 mL, white vinegar, plus milk to make), see Note	¾ cup	175 mL
Prepared orange juice	2 tbsp.	30 mL
Grated orange peel	1 tsp.	5 mL
Chopped dates	1 cup	250 mL

Measure first 7 ingredients into large bowl. Stir together thoroughly. Make a well in center.

Beat egg in small bowl until frothy. Mix in cooking oil, sour milk, orange juice, orange peel and dates. Pour into well in flour mixture. Stir just to moisten. Batter will be lumpy. Fill greased muffin cups ¾ full. Bake in 400°F (205°C) oven for 18 to 20 minutes until wooden pick inserted in several muffins comes out clean. Cool in pan for 5 minutes. Remove from pan to rack to cool completely. Makes 12 muffins.

1 muffin: 183 Calories; 5.7 g Total Fat; 242 mg Sodium; 3 g Protein; 33 g Carbohydrate; 3 g Dietary Fiber

Pictured on page 89.

Note: Buttermilk may be substituted for the sour milk.

ORANGE MUFFINS

A delicious orange flavor with little flecks of date throughout. Scrumptious!

Whole unpeeled orange	1	1
Prepared orange juice	½ cup	125 mL
Chopped dates	½ cup	125 mL
Large egg	1	1
Hard margarine (or butter), softened	½ cup	125 mL
All-purpose flour	1¾ cups	425 mL
Granulated sugar	¾ cup	175 mL
Baking powder	1 tsp.	5 mL
Baking soda	1 tsp.	5 mL

Cut orange into 8 pieces. Remove seeds. Combine orange pieces and juice in blender. Process until smooth. Add dates, egg and margarine. Process. Pour into medium bowl.

Measure flour, sugar, baking powder and baking soda into small bowl. Mix thoroughly. Pour over top of orange mixture. Stir just to moisten. Fill greased muffin cups ¾ full. Bake in 400°F (205°C) oven for 20 minutes until wooden pick inserted in several muffins comes out clean. Cool in pan for 5 minutes. Remove from pan to rack to cool completely. Makes 16 muffins.

1 muffin: 171 Calories; 6.6 g Total Fat; 163 mg Sodium; 2 g Protein; 27 g Carbohydrate; 1 g Dietary Fiber

CHIPPER MUFFINS

Double the chocolate flavor with cocoa and chocolate chips. Great snacking!

All-purpose flour	1¾ cups	425 mL
Granulated sugar	¾ cup	175 mL
Cocoa	⅓ cup	75 mL
Baking powder	1 tbsp.	15 mL
Salt	½ tsp.	2 mL
Semisweet chocolate chips	1 cup	250 mL
Large egg	1	1
Cooking oil	⅓ cup	75 mL
Milk	1 cup	250 mL
Vanilla	1 tsp.	5 mL

Measure first 6 ingredients into medium bowl. Stir thoroughly. Make a well in center.

Beat egg in small bowl. Add cooking oil, milk and vanilla. Pour into well in flour mixture. Stir just to moisten. Fill greased muffin cups ¾ full. Bake in 400°F (205°C) oven for about 20 minutes until wooden pick inserted in several muffins comes out clean. Cool in pan for 5 minutes. Remove from pan to rack to cool completely. Makes 12 muffins.

1 muffin: 263 Calories; 11.8 g Total Fat; 136 mg Sodium; 4 g Protein; 38 g Carbohydrate; 3 g Dietary Fiber

Pictured on page 17.

QUICK BREAD MUFFINS

A perfect meal-type muffin. These are not sweet.

Large egg	1	1
Milk	1 cup	250 mL
Cooking oil	¼ cup	60 mL
All-purpose flour	2 cups	500 mL
Granulated sugar	1½ tbsp.	25 mL
Baking powder	4 tsp.	20 mL
Salt	¾ tsp.	4 mL

Beat egg in medium bowl until frothy. Add milk and cooking oil. Mix.

Stir flour, sugar, baking powder and salt together in small bowl. Add to egg mixture. Stir just to moisten. Fill greased muffin cups ¾ full. Bake in 400°F (205°C) oven for about 20 minutes until wooden pick inserted in several muffins comes out clean. Cool in pan for 5 minutes. Remove from pan to rack to cool completely. Makes 12 muffins.

1 muffin: 147 Calories; 5.7 g Total Fat; 192 mg Sodium; 4 g Protein; 20 g Carbohydrate; 1 g Dietary Fiber

SPICED APPLE MUFFINS

First-class spicy muffins. Good apple flavor.

All-purpose flour	2 cups	500 mL
Flakes of bran cereal	1 cup	250 mL
Brown sugar, packed	⅔ cup	150 mL
Baking powder	1 tbsp.	15 mL
Salt	1 tsp.	5 mL
Ground cinnamon	½ tsp.	2 mL
Ground nutmeg	¼ tsp.	1 mL
Large eggs	2	2
Milk	⅔ cup	150 mL
Cooking oil	¼ cup	60 mL
Grated peeled apple	1 cup	250 mL

Combine flour, bran flakes, brown sugar, baking powder, salt, cinnamon and nutmeg in large bowl. Fluff together with fork to thoroughly distribute baking powder. Make a well in center.

Beat eggs together lightly in medium bowl. Add milk, cooking oil and apple. Stir together. Pour into well in flour mixture. Stir just to moisten. Batter will be lumpy. Fill greased muffin cups ¾ full. Bake in 400°F (205°C) oven for 15 to 20 minutes until wooden pick inserted in several muffins comes out clean. Cool in pan for 5 minutes. Remove from pan to rack to cool completely. Makes 16 muffins.

1 muffin: 159 Calories; 4.6 g Total Fat; 218 mg Sodium; 3 g Protein; 27 g Carbohydrate; 1 g Dietary Fiber

SIX-WEEK BRAN MUFFINS

Store batter in refrigerator. Bake a fresh supply every day if you like.

Flakes of bran cereal	4 cups	1 L
All-bran cereal	2 cups	500 mL
Boiling water	2 cups	500 mL
Hard margarine (or butter), softened	1 cup	250 mL
Granulated sugar	1½ cups	375 mL
Brown sugar, packed	1½ cups	375 mL
Large eggs	4	4
Buttermilk	4 cups	1 L
Cooking (or fancy) molasses (optional)	¼ cup	60 mL
All-purpose flour	5 cups	1.25 L
Baking soda	2 tbsp.	30 mL
Baking powder	1 tbsp.	15 mL
Salt	1 tsp.	5 mL
Raisins	2 cups	500 mL

Combine both cereals and boiling water in medium bowl. Let stand for about 10 minutes.

Cream margarine and both sugars together in large bowl. Add eggs, 1 at a time, beating well after each addition. Stir in buttermilk. Add molasses. Stir in cereal mixture.

Combine flour, baking soda, baking powder, salt and raisins in medium bowl. Mix thoroughly. Add to bran mixture. Stir just to moisten. Store in refrigerator; it will keep for 6 weeks. As required, fill greased muffin cups ¾ full. Bake in 400°F (205°C) oven for 20 to 25 minutes until wooden pick inserted in several muffins comes out clean. Cool in pan for 5 minutes. Remove from pan to rack to cool completely. Makes 48 muffins.

1 muffin: 195 Calories; 5 g Total Fat; 350 mg Sodium; 4 g Protein; 36 g Carbohydrate; 2 g Dietary Fiber

Variation: You may switch the amounts of bran cereal and bran flakes. Instead, use 2 cups (500 mL) bran flakes and 4 cups (1 L) all-bran cereal. Or, use natural bran to replace one cereal.

PINEAPPLE MUFFINS

Most and tender with a good pineapple flavor.

Cream cheese, softened	4 oz.	125 g
Granulated sugar	1 cup	250 mL
Large egg	1	1
Vanilla	1 tsp.	5 mL
Sour cream	½ cup	125 mL
Canned crushed pineapple, drained	19 oz.	540 mL
All-purpose flour	2 cups	500 mL
Baking soda	1 tsp.	5 mL
Salt	1 tsp.	5 mL

Beat cream cheese and sugar together in large bowl. Beat in egg and vanilla. Add sour cream. Mix. Stir in pineapple.

Stir flour, baking soda and salt together in small bowl. Add to pineapple mixture. Stir just to moisten. Fill greased muffin cups ¾ full. Bake in 350°F (175°C) oven for about 30 minutes until wooden pick inserted in several muffins comes out clean. Cool in pan for 5 minutes. Remove from pan to rack to cool completely. Make 16 muffins.

1 muffin: 167 Calories; 4.3 g Total Fat; 202 mg Sodium; 3 g Protein; 29 g Carbohydrate; 1 g Dietary Fiber

1. Currant Scones, page 98
2. Drop Cheese Biscuits, page 9
3. Beer Bread, page 32
4. Sour Cream Coffee Cake, page 26
5. Fun Buns, page 20
6. Blueberry Lemon Muffins, page 70
7. Orange Bran Muffins, page 86
8. Cheese And Bacon Muffins, page 81

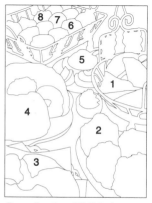

Props Courtesy Of: Eaton's; Stokes; The Basket House

GERM MUFFINS

It's the wheat "germ" that makes these muffins so good and so healthy.

Large egg	1	1
Granulated sugar	1/3 cup	75 mL
Brown sugar, packed	1/3 cup	75 mL
Cooking oil	1/3 cup	75 mL
Buttermilk (see Note)	1 cup	250 mL
Vanilla	1 tsp.	5 mL
All-purpose flour	1 1/4 cups	300 mL
Wheat germ	1 cup	250 mL
Baking powder	1 tsp.	5 mL
Baking soda	1 tsp.	5 mL
Salt	1/4 tsp.	1 mL

Mix first 6 ingredients in medium bowl.

Combine remaining 5 ingredients in large bowl. Stir to mix. Make a well in center. Pour egg mixture over flour mixture. Stir just to moisten. Fill greased muffin cups 3/4 full. Bake in 400°F (205°C) oven for about 12 minutes until wooden pick inserted in several muffins comes out clean. Cool in pan for 10 minutes. Remove from pan to rack to cool completely. Makes 12 muffins.

1 muffin: 206 Calories; 8.1 g Total Fat; 203 mg Sodium; 5 g Protein; 29 g Carbohydrate; 2 g Dietary Fiber

Note: Sour milk may be substituted for the buttermilk. To make sour milk, add 1 tbsp. (15 mL) white vinegar plus milk to make 1 cup (250 mL).

Variation: Add 1/2 cup (125 mL) raisins, chopped dates or blueberries.

BRAN GRAHAM MUFFINS

Must be the "Cadillac" of bran muffins. Nutty texture, chock-full of nutrition.

All-bran cereal	1 cup	250 mL
Graham cracker crumbs	1 cup	250 mL
All-purpose flour	1/2 cup	125 mL
Whole wheat (or all-purpose) flour	2 tbsp.	30 mL
Brown sugar, packed	1/4 cup	60 mL
Wheat germ	1/4 cup	60 mL
Baking soda	1 tsp.	5 mL
Salt	1/4 tsp.	1 mL
Coarsely chopped raisins	1/2 cup	125 mL
Large egg	1	1
Cooking oil	1/3 cup	75 mL
Cooking (or fancy) molasses	1/4 cup	60 mL
Buttermilk	3/4 cup	175 mL
Vanilla	1/2 tsp.	2 mL

Measure first 8 ingredients into large bowl. Mix well. Stir in raisins.

Beat egg in small bowl until frothy. Add cooking oil, molasses, buttermilk and vanilla. Beat to mix. Pour over flour mixture. Stir just to moisten. Fill greased muffin cups 3/4 full. Bake in 375°F (190°C) oven for 20 minutes until wooden pick inserted in several muffins comes out clean. Cool in pan for 5 minutes. Remove from pan to rack to cool completely. Makes 12 muffins.

1 muffin: 210 Calories; 8.3 g Total Fat; 314 mg Sodium; 4 g Protein; 33 g Carbohydrate; 3 g Dietary Fiber

If muffins are sticking to the pan, place the hot muffin pan on a wet towel. This will make the muffins easier to remove.

BABY APRICOT MUFFINS

An excellent, tender muffin that combines dried apricots and baby food.

All-purpose flour	1¾ cups	425 mL
Granulated sugar	½ cup	125 mL
Baking powder	2 tsp.	10 mL
Baking soda	½ tsp.	2 mL
Salt	½ tsp.	2 mL
Ground dried apricots	⅓ cup	75 mL
Large egg	1	1
Cooking oil	¼ cup	60 mL
Puréed apricots (baby food)	7½ oz.	213 mL

Measure first 6 ingredients into large bowl. Stir together well. Make a well in center.

Beat egg in small bowl until frothy. Mix in cooking oil and apricots. Pour into well in flour mixture. Stir just to moisten. Batter will be lumpy. Fill greased muffin cups ¾ full. Bake in 400°F (205°C) oven for 20 to 25 minutes until wooden pick inserted in several muffins comes out clean. Cool in pan for 5 minutes. Remove from pan to rack to cool completely. Makes 18 muffins.

1 muffin: 119 Calories; 3.7 g Total Fat; 122 mg Sodium; 2 g Protein; 20 g Carbohydrate; 1 g Dietary Fiber

CARROT PINEAPPLE MUFFINS

Golden with flecks of carrot and pineapple showing. Good all year round.

All-purpose flour	2 cups	500 mL
Granulated sugar	¾ cup	175 mL
Baking powder	1 tsp.	5 mL
Baking soda	1 tsp.	5 mL
Ground cinnamon	1 tsp.	5 mL
Salt	½ tsp.	2 mL
Large eggs, fork-beaten	2	2
Cooking oil	½ cup	125 mL
Finely grated carrot	1 cup	250 mL
Canned crushed pineapple, with juice	½ cup	125 mL
Vanilla	1 tsp.	5 mL

Mix first 6 ingredients in large bowl.

Add eggs, cooking oil, carrot, pineapple with juice and vanilla. Beat on low just to moisten. Fill greased muffin cups ⅔ full. Bake in 350°F (175°C) oven for 20 to 25 minutes until wooden pick inserted in several muffins comes out clean. Cool in pan for 5 minutes. Remove from pan to rack to cool completely. Makes 12 muffins.

1 muffin: 240 Calories; 10.7 g Total Fat; 243 mg Sodium; 3 g Protein; 33 g Carbohydrate; 1 g Dietary Fiber

DATE MUFFINS

Full of dates. Moist and yummy.

Chopped dates	1½ cups	375 mL
Boiling water	¾ cup	175 mL
Baking soda	1 tsp.	5 mL
All-purpose flour	1¾ cups	425 mL
Baking powder	1 tsp.	5 mL
Salt	½ tsp.	2 mL
Chopped walnuts	½ cup	125 mL
Large eggs	2	2
Brown sugar, packed	¾ cup	175 mL
Cooking oil	¼ cup	60 mL
Vanilla	1 tsp.	5 mL

Combine dates, boiling water and baking soda in small bowl. Set aside.

Combine flour, baking powder, salt and walnuts in second small bowl. Stir together well. Set aside.

Beat eggs in medium bowl until frothy. Slowly blend in brown sugar, cooking oil and vanilla. Stir in date mixture. Add flour mixture. Stir just to moisten. Batter may be lumpy. Fill greased muffin cups ¾ full. Bake in 400°F (205°C) oven for 20 to 25 minutes until wooden pick inserted in several muffins comes out clean. Cool in pan for 5 minutes. Remove from pan to rack to cool completely. Makes 16 muffins.

1 muffin: 202 Calories; 7 g Total Fat; 184 mg Sodium; 3 g Protein; 33 g Carbohydrate; 2 g Dietary Fiber

CHEESE BRAN MUFFINS

Just an excellent cheesy muffin.

All-bran cereal	1 cup	250 mL
Buttermilk (see Note)	1¼ cups	300 mL
Large egg	1	1
Cooking oil	¼ cup	60 mL
All-purpose flour	1½ cups	375 mL
Granulated sugar	¼ cup	60 mL
Baking powder	1½ tsp.	7 mL
Baking soda	½ tsp.	2 mL
Salt	½ tsp.	2 mL
Grated sharp Cheddar cheese	1 cup	250 mL

Combine cereal and buttermilk in small bowl.

Beat egg in medium bowl until frothy. Stir in cooking oil and cereal mixture.

Combine remaining 6 ingredients in large bowl. Make a well in center. Pour batter into well. Stir just to moisten. Batter will be lumpy. Fill greased muffin cups ¾ full. Bake in 400°F (205°C) oven for 20 to 25 minutes until wooden pick inserted in several muffins comes out clean. Cool in pan for 5 minutes. Serve warm. Makes 16 muffins.

1 muffin: 144 Calories; 6.8 g Total Fat; 241 mg Sodium; 5 g Protein; 17 g Carbohydrate; 2 g Dietary Fiber

FRUIT MUFFINS

A very moist muffin. Uses leftover fruit.

All-purpose flour	2 cups	500 mL
Baking powder	1 tsp.	5 mL
Baking soda	1 tsp.	5 mL
Salt	1 tsp.	5 mL
Hard margarine (or butter), softened	½ cup	125 mL
Granulated sugar	½ cup	125 mL
Large egg	1	1
Milk	1 cup	250 mL
Diced canned fruit (your choice), drained	¾ cup	175 mL

Mix flour, baking powder, baking soda and salt in large bowl. Make a well in center.

Cream margarine, sugar and egg together in medium bowl. Mix in milk and fruit. Pour into well in flour mixture. Stir just to moisten. Batter will be lumpy. Fill greased muffin cups ¾ full. Bake in 400°F (205°C) oven for 20 to 25 minutes until wooden pick inserted in several muffins comes out clean. Cool in pan for 5 minutes. Serve warm. Makes 16 muffins.

1 muffin: 156 Calories; 6.8 g Total Fat; 341 mg Sodium; 3 g Protein; 21 g Carbohydrate; 1 g Dietary Fiber

CHEESY ONION MUFFINS

Makes a nice breakfast muffin.

All-purpose flour	2 cups	500 mL
Dry onion soup mix (stir before measuring)	1 tbsp.	15 mL
Granulated sugar	1½ tbsp.	25 mL
Baking powder	2 tsp.	10 mL
Baking soda	½ tsp.	2 mL
Grated sharp Cheddar cheese	1 cup	250 mL
Salt	¼ tsp.	1 mL
Large egg	1	1
Cooking oil	⅓ cup	75 mL
Milk	1 cup	250 mL

Measure first 7 ingredients into large bowl. Stir together. Make a well in center.

Beat egg in small bowl. Mix in cooking oil and milk. Stir. Pour into well in flour mixture. Stir just to moisten. Fill greased muffin cups almost full. Bake in 400°F (205°C) oven for 15 to 20 minutes. Cool in pan for 5 minutes. Remove from pan to rack to cool completely. Makes 12 muffins.

1 muffin: 203 Calories; 10.6 g Total Fat; 307 mg Sodium; 6 g Protein; 21 g Carbohydrate; 1 g Dietary Fiber

FILLED MUFFINS

Make two kinds of muffins with this recipe. Cream cheese mixed with jam is excellent too!

Large egg	1	1
Granulated sugar	3 tbsp.	50 mL
Cooking oil	¼ cup	60 mL
Milk	1 cup	250 mL
All-purpose flour	2 cups	500 mL
Baking powder	1 tbsp.	15 mL
Salt	½ tsp.	2 mL
Light cream cheese, shaped into 1 tsp. (5 mL) balls	6 tsp.	30 mL
Raspberry (or blackberry or black currant) jam	6 tsp.	30 mL

Beat egg, sugar and cooking oil together in small bowl until blended. Add milk. Mix.

Measure flour, baking powder and salt into large bowl. Stir together. Make a well in center. Pour milk mixture into well. Stir just to moisten. Divide ½ of batter among 12 greased muffin cups.

Place cream cheese balls on top in center of 6. Drop 1 tsp. (5 mL) jam in center of other 6. Divide remaining batter over top of all 12. Bake in 400°F (205°C) oven for 15 to 20 minutes until browned and wooden pick inserted in several muffins comes out clean. Cool in pan for 5 minutes. Remove from pan to rack to cool completely. Makes 12 muffins.

1 muffin: 166 Calories; 6.1 g Total Fat; 158 mg Sodium; 4 g Protein; 24 g Carbohydrate; 1 g Dietary Fiber

FRUITED MUFFINS

Spicy and colorful.

All-purpose flour	2 cups	500 mL
Baking powder	1 tsp.	5 mL
Baking soda	1 tsp.	5 mL
Salt	¾ tsp.	4 mL
Ground cinnamon	1 tsp.	5 mL
Raisins	½ cup	125 mL
Glazed mixed fruit	½ cup	125 mL
Hard margarine (or butter), softened	½ cup	125 mL
Granulated sugar	¾ cup	175 mL
Large egg	1	1
Buttermilk	1 cup	250 mL
Vanilla	½ tsp.	2 mL

Mix first 7 ingredients in large bowl. Make a well in center.

Cream margarine, sugar and egg together in small bowl. Mix in buttermilk and vanilla. Pour into well in flour mixture. Stir just to moisten. Batter will be lumpy. Fill greased muffin cups ¾ full. Bake in 400°F (205°C) oven for 20 to 25 minutes until wooden pick inserted in several muffins comes out clean. Cool in pan for 5 minutes. Serve warm. Makes 18 muffins.

1 muffin: 178 Calories; 6 g Total Fat; 277 mg Sodium; 3 g Protein; 29 g Carbohydrate; 1 g Dietary Fiber

Variation: Mix enough water or milk with ¾ cup (175 mL) icing (confectioner's) sugar to make a thin glaze. Drizzle over muffins.

Most muffin recipes state to "stir just to moisten." Over-stirring will cause muffins to peak very high and be tough in texture. Do not stir batter as you are filling the muffin cups.

CARROT BRAN MUFFINS

The pineapple makes this muffin tender and very moist.

All-purpose flour	1½ cups	375 mL
Brown sugar, packed	¾ cup	175 mL
Natural bran	¾ cup	175 mL
Baking powder	1 tsp.	5 mL
Baking soda	1 tsp.	5 mL
Salt	½ tsp.	2 mL
Ground cinnamon	1 tsp.	5 mL
Large eggs	2	2
Cooking oil	½ cup	125 mL
Grated carrot	1 cup	250 mL
Canned crushed pineapple, with juice	1 cup	250 mL

Mix first 7 ingredients in large bowl. Make a well in center.

Beat eggs together in medium bowl until frothy. Add cooking oil, carrot and pineapple with juice. Pour into well in flour mixture. Stir just to moisten. Batter will be lumpy. Fill greased muffin cups ¾ full. Bake in 400°F (205°C) oven for 20 to 25 minutes until wooden pick inserted in several muffins comes out clean. Cool in pan for 5 minutes. Remove from pan to rack to cool completely. Makes 14 muffins.

1 muffin: 205 Calories; 9.3 g Total Fat; 212 mg Sodium; 3 g Protein; 29 g Carbohydrate; 2 g Dietary Fiber

CARROT MUFFINS: Omit bran. Add 2 cups (500 mL) all-purpose flour.

PINEAPPLE MUFFINS

A delicately flavored, fine textured muffin.

All-purpose flour	2 cups	500 mL
Granulated sugar	½ cup	125 mL
Baking powder	1 tbsp.	15 mL
Salt	½ tsp.	2 mL
Large egg	1	1
Cooking oil	¼ cup	60 mL
Milk	1 cup	250 mL
Canned crushed, pineapple, well drained	½ cup	125 mL

Measure flour, sugar, baking powder and salt into large bowl. Stir. Make a well in center.

Beat egg in small bowl until frothy. Mix in cooking oil, milk and pineapple. Pour into well in flour mixture. Stir just to moisten. Batter will be lumpy. Fill greased muffin cups ¾ full. Bake in 400°F (205°C) oven for 20 to 25 minutes until wooden pick inserted in several muffins comes out clean. Cool in pan for 5 minutes. Serve warm. Makes 18 muffins.

1 muffin: 118 Calories; 3.8 g Total Fat; 89 mg Sodium; 2 g Protein; 19 g Carbohydrate; 1 g Dietary Fiber

BANANA DATE MUFFINS

Flavors combine well in this perky muffin.

All-purpose flour	2 cups	500 mL
Granulated sugar	2 tbsp.	30 mL
Baking powder	1 tbsp.	15 mL
Salt	1 tsp.	5 mL
Large egg, fork-beaten	1	1
Hard margarine (or butter), melted	¼ cup	60 mL
Milk	1 cup	250 mL
Chopped dates	⅔ cup	150 mL
Diced banana	⅔ cup	150 mL

Combine flour, sugar, baking powder and salt in large bowl. Stir. Make a well in center.

Beat egg in medium bowl until frothy. Mix in margarine, milk, dates and banana. Pour into well in flour mixture. Stir just to moisten. Batter will be lumpy. Fill greased muffin cups ¾ full. Bake in 400°F (205°C) oven for 20 to 25 minutes until wooden pick inserted in several muffins comes out clean. Cool in pan for 5 minutes. Serve warm. Makes 16 muffins.

1 muffin: 131 Calories; 3.5 g Total Fat; 218 mg Sodium; 3 g Protein; 22 g Carbohydrate; 1 g Dietary Fiber

★★★★★★★★★★★★★★★★★★★★★★★★★★★★★★★★★★

Scones

*W*hether you say "skahn" or "skon," these special recipes are sure to delight. Serve *Currant Scones*, page 98, warm from the oven and topped with butter, peanut butter or your favorite jam or marmalade. Place a basket of *Scottish Oat Scones*, page 96, on the table along with the peanut butter. For a taste sensation, combine cream cheese and a wedge of *King Scone*, page 95. These sweet and savory scones are just perfect at breakfast time, tea time or any time.

KING SCONE

A cream cheese and raisin filling is the special treat for this scone. Decadent.

Cream cheese, softened	8 oz.	250 g
Granulated sugar	½ cup	125 mL
Raisins (or currants)	½ cup	125 mL
Grated lemon peel	1 tsp.	5 mL
All-purpose flour	3 cups	750 mL
Baking powder	4 tsp.	20 mL
Salt	1 tsp.	5 mL
Hard margarine (or butter)	½ cup	125 mL
Large egg	1	1
Milk	1 cup	250 mL
Granulated sugar, sprinkle		

Beat cream cheese and sugar together well in small bowl. Stir in raisins and lemon peel. Set aside.

Measure flour, baking powder and salt into large bowl. Cut in margarine until fine and crumbly. Make a well in center.

Beat egg in second small bowl. Add milk. Stir. Pour into well in flour mixture. Stir with fork to form soft dough. Do not knead. Divide dough into 4 equal portions. Pat each portion into 6 inch (15 cm) circle. Place 2 circles on greased baking sheet. Spread cheese mixture over top. Cover with other 2 circles. Score each top into 8 wedges.

Sprinkle lightly with sugar. Bake in 425°F (220°C) oven for 15 to 20 minutes until risen and golden. Each scone cuts into 8 wedges.

1 wedge: 252 Calories; 12.3 g Total Fat; 305 mg Sodium; 5 g Protein; 31 g Carbohydrate; 1 g Dietary Fiber

RICH SCONES

So easy to make you can whip them up at a moment's notice.

All-purpose flour	2 cups	500 mL
Granulated sugar	½ cup	125 mL
Baking powder	1 tbsp.	15 mL
Salt	½ tsp.	2 mL
Hard margarine (or butter)	½ cup	125 mL
Large egg	1	1
Milk	⅔ cup	150 mL
Milk, for brushing tops		
Granulated sugar, for sprinkling		

Mix flour, sugar, baking powder and salt in large bowl. Cut in margarine until mixture is crumbly.

Beat egg lightly in small bowl. Add milk. Pour into flour mixture. Stir with fork to make soft dough. Pat into two 6 inch (15 cm) circles on greased baking sheet. Score each top into 6 wedges.

Brush tops with milk. Sprinkle with sugar. Bake in 425°F (220°C) oven for 15 minutes until risen and golden brown. Each scone cuts into 6 wedges.

1 wedge: 200 Calories; 8.9 g Total Fat; 226 mg Sodium; 3 g Protein; 27 g Carbohydrate; 1 g Dietary Fiber

SCOTTISH OAT SCONES

Nibble on these or have for lunch. They won't last long.

All-purpose flour	1½ cups	375 mL
Rolled oats (not instant)	2 cups	500 mL
Granulated sugar	¼ cup	60 mL
Baking powder	4 tsp.	20 mL
Salt	½ tsp.	2 mL
Currants	½ cup	125 mL
Large egg, fork-beaten	1	1
Hard margarine (or butter), melted	½ cup	125 mL
Milk	⅓ cup	75 mL
Granulated sugar, sprinkle		

Mix first 6 ingredients in large bowl. Make a well in center.

Beat egg in small bowl until frothy. Mix in margarine and milk. Pour into well in flour mixture. Stir with fork to make soft dough. Do not knead. Pat into two 6 to 7 inch (15 to 18 cm) circles. Transfer to greased baking sheet. Score each top into 8 wedges.

Sprinkle with sugar. Bake in 425°F (220°C) oven for 15 minutes until risen and golden. Each scone cuts into 8 wedges.

1 wedge: 170 Calories; 6.8 g Total Fat; 162 mg Sodium; 4 g Protein; 24 g Carbohydrate; 2 g Dietary Fiber

Be careful not to add too much extra flour when kneading the dough for your scones, or the resulting texture will be dry.

SAVORY SCONES

This one will get rave reviews all around the lunch table. Onion topping is excellent.

TOPPING

Hard margarine (or butter)	2 tbsp.	30 mL
Medium onions, halved lengthwise and thinly sliced	2	2
Ground rosemary	1 tsp.	5 mL
Ground thyme, generous measure	¼ tsp.	1 mL
Brown sugar, packed	1 tbsp.	15 mL

SCONE

All-purpose flour	3 cups	750 mL
Granulated sugar	1 tbsp.	15 mL
Baking powder	4 tsp.	20 mL
Baking soda	½ tsp.	2 mL
Salt	¾ tsp.	4 mL
Dried whole oregano	1 tsp.	5 mL
Garlic powder	¼ tsp.	1 mL
Dried sweet basil	¼ tsp.	1 mL
Hard margarine (or butter)	6 tbsp.	100 mL
Large egg, fork-beaten	1	1
Buttermilk	1 cup	250 mL

Topping: Melt margarine in frying pan. Add onion. Sauté until onion is clear and soft. Remove from heat.

Add rosemary, thyme and brown sugar. Stir.

Scone: Measure first 8 ingredients into large bowl. Cut in margarine until mixture is crumbly.

Add egg and buttermilk. Stir with fork to make soft dough. Turn out onto lightly floured surface. Knead 6 times. Pat into 2 circles, about ½ inch (12 mm) thick, on greased baking sheet. Score each top into 6 wedges. Spread onion mixture over top. Bake in 425°F (220°C) oven for 20 to 25 minutes until risen and golden. Each scone cuts into 6 wedges.

1 wedge: 224 Calories; 8.8 g Total Fat; 354 mg Sodium; 5 g Protein; 31 g Carbohydrate; 1 g Dietary Fiber

GRAHAM SCONES

Satisfies any appetite. Serve warm with jam.

All-purpose flour	1¼ cups	300 mL
Graham cracker crumbs	1 cup	250 mL
Rolled oats (not instant)	½ cup	125 mL
Granulated sugar	¼ cup	60 mL
Baking powder	4 tsp.	20 mL
Salt	½ tsp.	2 mL
Hard margarine (or butter)	½ cup	125 mL
Currants	½ cup	125 mL
Large egg	1	1
Milk	½ cup	125 mL

Milk, for brushing tops
Granulated sugar, for sprinkling

Combine first 6 ingredients in large bowl. Stir well. Cut in margarine until mixture is crumbly.

Stir in currants.

Beat egg in small bowl. Stir in milk. Add to flour mixture. Stir with fork to make soft dough. Turn out onto lightly floured surface. Knead lightly 10 times. Pat into two 6 inch (15 cm) circles on greased baking sheet. Score each top into 6 wedges.

Brush with milk. Sprinkle with sugar. Bake in 425°F (220°C) oven for 15 minutes until risen and golden. Each scone cuts into 6 wedges.

1 wedge: 220 Calories; 10 g Total Fat; 290 mg Sodium; 4 g Protein; 30 g Carbohydrate; 1 g Dietary Fiber

CURRANT SCONES

Just right for a morning coffee party.

All-purpose flour	2 cups	500 mL
Granulated sugar	¼ cup	60 mL
Baking powder	4 tsp.	20 mL
Salt	½ tsp.	2 mL
Hard margarine (or butter)	¼ cup	60 mL
Currants	½ cup	125 mL
Large egg	1	1
Milk	⅔ cup	150 mL

Milk, for brushing tops
Granulated sugar, for sprinkling

Combine flour, sugar, baking powder and salt in large bowl. Cut in margarine until mixture is crumbly. Stir in currants. Make a well in center.

Beat egg in small bowl until frothy. Stir in milk. Pour into well in flour mixture. Stir with fork to make soft dough. Turn out onto lightly floured surface. Knead 8 to 10 times. Pat into two 6 inch (15 cm) circles on greased baking sheet. Score each top into 6 wedges.

Brush tops with milk. Sprinkle with sugar. Bake in 425°F (220°C) oven for 15 minutes until risen and golden. Each scone cuts into 6 wedges.

1 wedge: 165 Calories; 4.9 g Total Fat; 180 mg Sodium; 4 g Protein; 27 g Carbohydrate; 1 g Dietary Fiber

Pictured on page 89.

BRAN CEREAL SCONES: Use only 1⅓ cups (325 mL) all-purpose flour and add 1 cup (250 mL) flakes of bran cereal.

CHEESE SCONES: Add 1 cup (250 mL) grated Cheddar cheese.

FRUIT SCONES: Omit currants. Add 1 cup (250 mL) glazed mixed fruit.

ORANGE SCONES: Add 1 tbsp. (15 mL) grated orange peel.

YOGURT SCONES: Omit milk. Add ¾ cup (175 mL) plain yogurt.

WHOLE WHEAT SCONES: Substitute ½ of all-purpose flour with whole wheat flour.

BRAN SCONES

Sugar adds to the flavor but can be omitted.

All-purpose flour	1¾ cups	425 mL
Natural bran (or all-bran cereal)	½ cup	125 mL
Granulated sugar	¼ cup	60 mL
Baking powder	1 tbsp.	15 mL
Salt	1 tsp.	5 mL
Hard margarine (or butter)	¼ cup	60 mL
Large egg	1	1
Milk	¾ cup	175 mL

Milk, for brushing tops
Granulated sugar, for sprinkling

Combine flour, bran, sugar, baking powder and salt in large bowl. Cut in margarine until mixture is crumbly.

Beat egg in small bowl. Mix in milk. Pour into flour mixture. Stir to make soft dough. Knead gently 8 to 10 times on lightly floured surface. Pat into two 6 inch (15 cm) circles on greased baking sheet. Score each top into 6 wedges.

Brush tops with milk. Sprinkle with sugar. Bake in 425°F (220°C) oven for 15 minutes until risen and golden. Each scone cuts into 6 wedges.

1 wedge: 144 Calories; 5 g Total Fat; 292 mg Sodium; 4 g Protein; 22 g Carbohydrate; 2 g Dietary Fiber

SPICY SCONES

Greet your guests with the aroma of these scones fresh from the oven.

All-purpose flour	1 cup	250 mL
Whole wheat flour	1 cup	250 mL
Granulated sugar	¼ cup	60 mL
Baking powder	4 tsp.	20 mL
Ground cinnamon	1½ tsp.	7 mL
Ground nutmeg	½ tsp.	2 mL
Salt	½ tsp.	2 mL
Hard margarine (or butter)	⅓ cup	75 mL
Raisins (or currants)	½ cup	125 mL
Large egg	1	1
Milk	¾ cup	175 mL

Milk, for brushing tops
Granulated sugar, for
    sprinkling

Combine first 7 ingredients in large bowl. Cut in margarine until crumbly. Stir in raisins. Make a well in center.

Beat egg in small bowl until frothy. Mix in milk. Pour into well in flour mixture. Stir to make soft dough. Turn out onto lightly floured surface. Knead gently 8 to 10 times. Pat into two 6 inch (15 cm) circles on greased baking sheet. Score each top into 6 wedges

Brush tops with milk. Sprinkle with sugar. Bake in 425°F (220°C) oven for 15 minutes until risen and golden. Serve hot with butter. Each scone cuts into 6 wedges.

1 wedge: 177 Calories; 6.4 g Total Fat; 197 mg Sodium; 4 g Protein; 27 g Carbohydrate; 2 g Dietary Fiber

BREAKFAST SCONES

These are shaped to allow each to hold two poached eggs. Decrease baking time if you choose to make smaller scones.

All-purpose flour	2 cups	500 mL
Baking powder	4 tsp.	20 mL
Granulated sugar	2 tsp.	10 mL
Salt	½ tsp.	2 mL
Hard margarine (or butter)	¼ cup	60 mL
Milk	¾ cup	175 mL

Combine first 4 ingredients in medium bowl. Stir. Cut in margarine until mixture is crumbly.

Add milk. Stir to form soft dough. Turn out onto lightly floured surface. Knead 8 times. Divide dough into 6 equal portions. Press each portion into 3 × 5 inch (7.5 × 12.5 cm) rectangle. Since this dough tends to rise more in center, make center a bit thinner than sides. Arrange on ungreased baking sheet. Bake in 425°F (220°C) oven for about 15 minutes. Makes 6 scones.

1 scone: 256 Calories; 8.9 g Total Fat; 338 mg Sodium; 6 g Protein; 38 g Carbohydrate; 1 g Dietary Fiber

---

Most scone recipes are easily doubled, but don't crowd the oven. Bake one sheet at a time and be sure that the oven has returned to the correct temperature before adding the next batch.

GINGER SCONES

Very tasty and dark. Out of the ordinary.

All-purpose flour	2 cups	500 mL
Granulated sugar	1 tbsp.	15 mL
Baking powder	2 tsp.	10 mL
Baking soda	½ tsp.	2 mL
Salt	¾ tsp.	4 mL
Ground cinnamon	½ tsp.	2 mL
Ground ginger	½ tsp.	2 mL
Hard margarine (or butter)	¼ cup	60 mL
Large egg	1	1
Cooking (or fancy) molasses	¼ cup	60 mL
Buttermilk (see Note)	½ cup	125 mL

Milk, for brushing tops
Granulated sugar, for
    sprinkling

Measure first 7 ingredients into large bowl. Stir. Cut in margarine until crumbly. Make a well in center.

Beat egg in small bowl until frothy. Mix in molasses and buttermilk. Pour into well in flour mixture. Stir with fork to make soft dough. Turn out onto lightly floured surface. Knead gently 8 to 10 times. Pat into two 6 inch (15 cm) circles on greased baking sheet. Score each top into 6 wedges.

Brush tops with milk. Sprinkle with sugar. Bake in 425°F (220°C) oven until risen and golden. Each scone cuts into 6 wedges.

1 wedge: 151 Calories; 4.8 g Total Fat; 296 mg Sodium; 3 g Protein; 24 g Carbohydrate; 1 g Dietary Fiber

Note: Sour milk may be substituted for the buttermilk. To make sour milk, add 2 tsp. (10 mL) white vinegar to milk to make ½ cup (125 mL).

BUTTERMILK SCONES: Omit cinnamon, ginger and molasses. Add ⅔ cup (150 mL) buttermilk.

SOUR CREAM SCONES: Omit cinnamon, ginger and molasses. Substitute ¾ cup (175 mL) sour cream for the buttermilk.

APPLE SCONES

Terrific aroma. Terrific taste. Perfect for tea time.

All-purpose flour	2 cups	500 mL
Granulated sugar	¼ cup	60 mL
Baking powder	2 tsp.	10 mL
Baking soda	½ tsp.	2 mL
Salt	½ tsp.	2 mL
Hard margarine (or butter)	¼ cup	60 mL
Large apple, peeled and grated	1	1
Milk	½ cup	125 mL

Milk, for brushing tops
Sugar, for sprinkling
Ground cinnamon, for
    sprinkling

Measure flour, sugar, baking powder, baking soda and salt into large bowl. Cut in margarine until mixture is crumbly.

Add apple and milk. Stir with fork to form soft dough. Turn out onto lightly floured surface. Knead gently 8 to 10 times. Pat into two 6 inch (15 cm) circles on greased baking sheet. Score each top into 6 wedges.

Brush tops with milk. Sprinkle with sugar and cinnamon. Bake in 425°F (220°C) oven for 15 minutes until risen and golden. Each scone cuts into 6 wedges.

1 wedge: 145 Calories; 4.5 g Total Fat; 227 mg Sodium; 3 g Protein; 24 g Carbohydrate; 1 g Dietary Fiber

Pictured on page 53 and on back cover.

CURRANT APPLE SCONES: Add ½ cup (125 mL) currants to batter.

Measurement Tables

T hroughout this book measurements are given in Conventional and Metric measure. To compensate for differences between the two measurements due to rounding, a full metric measure is not always used. The cup used is the standard 8 fluid ounce. Temperature is given in degrees Fahrenheit and Celsius. Baking pan measurements are in inches and centimetres as well as quarts and litres. An exact metric conversion is given below as well as the working equivalent (Standard Measure).

OVEN TEMPERATURES

Fahrenheit (°F)	Celsius (°C)
175°	80°
200°	95°
225°	110°
250°	120°
275°	140°
300°	150°
325°	160°
350°	175°
375°	190°
400°	205°
425°	220°
450°	230°
475°	240°
500°	260°

SPOONS

Conventional Measure	Metric Exact Conversion Millilitre (mL)	Metric Standard Measure Millilitre (mL)
1/8 teaspoon (tsp.)	0.6 mL	0.5 mL
1/4 teaspoon (tsp.)	1.2 mL	1 mL
1/2 teaspoon (tsp.)	2.4 mL	2 mL
1 teaspoon (tsp.)	4.7 mL	5 mL
2 teaspoons (tsp.)	9.4 mL	10 mL
1 tablespoon (tbsp.)	14.2 mL	15 mL

CUPS

1/4 cup (4 tbsp.)	56.8 mL	60 mL
1/3 cup (5 1/3 tbsp.)	75.6 mL	75 mL
1/2 cup (8 tbsp.)	113.7 mL	125 mL
2/3 cup (10 2/3 tbsp.)	151.2 mL	150 mL
3/4 cup (12 tbsp.)	170.5 mL	175 mL
1 cup (16 tbsp.)	227.3 mL	250 mL
4 1/2 cups	1022.9 mL	1000 mL (1 L)

PANS

Conventional Inches	Metric Centimetres
8x8 inch	20x20 cm
9x9 inch	22x22 cm
9x13 inch	22x33 cm
10x15 inch	25x38 cm
11x17 inch	28x43 cm
8x2 inch round	20x5 cm
9x2 inch round	22x5 cm
10x4 1/2 inch tube	25x11 cm
8x4x3 inch loaf	20x10x7.5 cm
9x5x3 inch loaf	22x12.5x7.5 cm

DRY MEASUREMENTS

Conventional Measure Ounces (oz.)	Metric Exact Conversion Grams (g)	Metric Standard Measure Grams (g)
1 oz.	28.3 g	28 g
2 oz.	56.7 g	57 g
3 oz.	85.0 g	85 g
4 oz.	113.4 g	125 g
5 oz.	141.7 g	140 g
6 oz.	170.1 g	170 g
7 oz.	198.4 g	200 g
8 oz.	226.8 g	250 g
16 oz.	453.6 g	500 g
32 oz.	907.2 g	1000 g (1 kg)

CASSEROLES (CANADA & BRITAIN)

Standard Size Casserole	Exact Metric Measure
1 qt. (5 cups)	1.13 L
1 1/2 qts. (7 1/2 cups)	1.69 L
2 qts. (10 cups)	2.25 L
2 1/2 qts. (12 1/2 cups)	2.81 L
3 qts. (15 cups)	3.38 L
4 qts. (20 cups)	4.5 L
5 qts. (25 cups)	5.63 L

CASSEROLES (UNITED STATES)

Standard Size Casserole	Exact Metric Measure
1 qt. (4 cups)	900 mL
1 1/2 qts. (6 cups)	1.35 L
2 qts. (8 cups)	1.8 L
2 1/2 qts. (10 cups)	2.25 L
3 qts. (12 cups)	2.7 L
4 qts. (16 cups)	3.6 L
5 qts. (20 cups)	4.5 L

Index

Mail Order Form

See reverse for list of cookbooks

EXCLUSIVE MAIL ORDER OFFER
Buy 2 Get 1 FREE!
Buy any 2 cookbooks—choose a **3rd FREE** of equal or less value than the lowest price paid.

QUANTITY	CODE	TITLE	PRICE EACH	PRICE TOTAL
			$	$
	TOTAL BOOKS (including FREE)			

DON'T FORGET to indicate your FREE book(s). (see exclusive mail order offer above) PLEASE PRINT

TOTAL BOOKS PURCHASED: $

	INTERNATIONAL		CANADA & USA	
Plus Shipping & Handling (PER DESTINATION)	$ 7.00	(one book)	$ 5.00	(1-3 books)
Additional Books (INCLUDING FREE BOOKS)	$	($2.00 each)	$	($1.00 each)
SUB-TOTAL	$		$	
Canadian residents add G.S.T(7%)			$	
TOTAL AMOUNT ENCLOSED	$		$	

The Fine Print

- Orders outside Canada must be **PAID IN US FUNDS** by cheque or money order drawn on Canadian or US bank or by credit card.
- Make cheque or money order payable to: **COMPANY'S COMING PUBLISHING LIMITED.**
- Prices are expressed in Canadian dollars for Canada, US dollars for USA & International and are subject to change without prior notice.
- Orders are shipped surface mail. For courier rates, visit our web-site: **www.companyscoming.com** or contact us: **Tel: (780) 450-6223 Fax: (780) 450-1857.**
- Sorry, no C.O.D's.

☐ MasterCard   ☐ VISA _____
Expiry date

Account # _____

Name of cardholder _____

Cardholder's signature _____

Shipping Address
Send the cookbooks listed above to:

Name: _____

Street: _____

City: _____   Prov./State: _____

Country: _____   Postal Code/Zip: _____

Tel: (___) _____

E-mail address: _____

Gift Giving

- Let us help you with your gift giving!
- We will send cookbooks directly to the recipients of your choice if you give us their names and addresses.
- Please specify the titles you wish to send to each person.
- If you would like to include your personal note or card, we will be pleased to enclose it with your gift order.
- Company's Coming Cookbooks make excellent gifts: Birthdays, bridal showers, Mother's Day, Father's Day, graduation or any occasion... collect them all!

Company's Coming cookbooks are available at retail locations *THROUGHOUT* Canada!

See reverse for mail order

Assorted Titles	CA$19.99 Canada	US$19.99 USA & International

CODE	
EE	Easy Entertaining* (hardcover)
BE	Beef Today!

Buy any 2 cookbooks—choose a 3rd FREE of equal or less value than the lowest price paid.

Assorted Titles	CA$14.99 Canada	US$12.99 USA & International

CODE		CODE	
LFC	Low-fat Cooking*	SN	Kids-Snacks*
LFP	Low-fat Pasta*	KLU	Kids-Lunches

Buy any 2 cookbooks—choose a 3rd FREE of equal or less value than the lowest price paid.   *Available in French

Original Series	CA$12.99 Canada	US$10.99 USA & International

CODE		CODE		CODE		CODE	
SQ	150 Delicious Squares*	CO	Cookies*	PI	Pies*	BR	Breads*
CA	Casseroles*	VE	Vegetables	LR	Light Recipes*	ME	Meatless Cooking*
MU	Muffins & More*	MC	Main Courses	MI	Microwave Cooking*	CT	Cooking For Two*
SA	Salads*	PA	Pasta*	PR	Preserves*	BB	Breakfasts & Brunches*
AP	Appetizers	CK	Cakes	LCA	Light Casseroles*	SC	Slow Cooker Recipes
DE	Desserts	BA	Barbecues*	CH	Chicken, Etc.*	PZ	Pizza!*
SS	Soups & Sandwiches	DI	Dinners of the World	KC	Kids Cooking*	ODM	One-Dish Meals* ◀NEW▶
HE	Holiday Entertaining*	LU	Lunches*	FS	Fish & Seafood*		Aug. '99

Buy any 2 cookbooks—choose a 3rd FREE of equal or less value than the lowest price paid.   *Available in French

Select Series	CA$9.99 Canada US$7.99 USA & International	Greatest Hits

CODE		CODE		CODE	◀NEW▶ Apr. '99
GB	Ground Beef*	TMM	30-Minute Meals*	BML	Biscuits, Muffins & Loaves*
B&R	Beans & Rice*	MAS	Make-Ahead Salads	DSD	Dips, Spreads & Dressings*
S&M	Sauces & Marinades*	NBD	No-Bake Desserts		

Buy any 2 cookbooks—choose a 3rd FREE of equal or less value than the lowest price paid.   *Available in French

visit our web-site!
www.companyscoming.com

Company's Coming
COOKBOOKS

Company's Coming Publishing Limited
2311 - 96 Street
Edmonton, Alberta, Canada T6N 1G3
Tel: (780) 450-6223 Fax: (780) 450-1857
www.companyscoming.com

yES! Please send a catalogue.
❏ English ❏ French